House of Quality (QFD) in a Minute

Christian N. Madu, Ph.D.

Research Professor and Chair
Management Science Program
Co-Editor, International Journal of Quality & Reliability
Management
Department of Management and Management Science
Lubin School of Business
Pace University
New York, USA

CHI PUBLISHERS
FAIRFIELD, CT

House of Quality

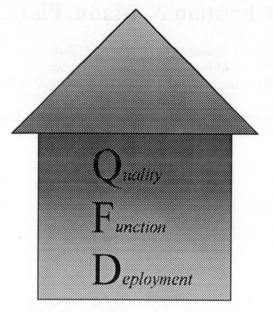

in a Minute

Christian N. Madu, Ph.D.

© Chi Publishers

A C.I.P. Catalogue record for this book is available from the Library of Congress

Library of Congress Catalog Card Number: 99-96210
ISBN 0-9676023-0-0

Published by Chi Publishers.
P.O. Box 1171, Fairfield, CT 06432

Sold and distributed by Chi Publishers
P.O. Box 1171, Fairfield, CT 06432
Telephone: 203-261-0739
Email: chipublishers@aol.com

First published in the United States in 2000

Contents

Contents

PREFACE

The *House of Quality (QFD) in a Minute* is written with two major objectives. First, to introduce the reader to the basics of quality function deployment (QFD) which is now widely used in major corporations and second, to get the practitioner ready to use QFD without extensive training and seminars that may end up being very costly. In this book, we have demonstrated in simple form how other techniques such as the analytic hierarchy process (AHP) can be used within the QFD chart. It is also important that the reader understands the role of QFD within the overall quality imperative of a firm. As a result, we have added chapters to demonstrate the link between QFD and other important quality programs such as quality control charts and concurrent engineering. QFD is also shown to be part of the organisation's business strategy. The need to integrate QFD within the firm's strategic plan is also demonstrated in the book. Evidently, the driving force behind the use of QFD is to help the firm to design products and services that satisfy customer requirements by listening to the voice of the customer. We have also shown that through the application of QFD, a firm can improve its productivity, control costs, increase market share, remain in business and remain competitive.

Another major feature of this book can be seen from its title, *House of Quality* in a Minute. It is precise and direct. The reader with no knowledge of the topic can read this entire book in a couple of hours and begin to apply the concepts. After reading the book, some may even develop interest in QFD and seek more advanced books. However, it is important that readers don't spend exorbitantly to decide if they are interested in QFD. This book is the right place to start and can be used as a handbook or a quick reference manual. In fact, many Japanese managers resort to basic books such as this to understand the emerging management tools and techniques that have helped them to become competitive.

Finally, I will like to thank all those who have helped me in preparing this manuscript especially my brother, Ernest C. Madu and my sister-in-law, Ms. Benardine Agocha who took out time from their busy schedules to review this "book" and my graduate research assistant Olalere Odusote who worked very hard to prepare the final copy of the book for the publisher. I thank all the authors with whom I have had the privilege to work in developing the Handbook of Total Quality Management and as the editor of the *International Journal of Quality Science,* and as co-editor of the *International Journal of Quality and Reliability Management Journal.* The experience I have gained over these years in doing these projects, made me believe that there is a need for a succinct and direct books on important quality and management tools.

Christian N. Madu
Pace University,
New York.

Biographical sketch

Christian N. Madu is research professor and chair of the management science program at the Lubin School of Business, Pace University. He is the author/co-author of more than 80 research papers in several areas of operations research, management science, quality management and management. His research publications have appeared in several journals including *Quality Management Journal, Decision Sciences, International Journal of Quality Science, International Journal of Quality and Reliability Management, Futures, Long Range Planning, European Journal of Operational Research, OMEGA, IIE Transactions, Applied Mathematics Letters, Mathematical and Computer Modeling, Socio-economic Planning Sciences, Journal of Operational Society, International Journal of Production Research, Computers and Operations Research,* and several others. He is the author/co-author or editor of seven published books including *Handbook of Total Quality Management* (Kluwer Academic Publishers 1998), *Managing Green Technologies for Global Competitiveness* (Quorum Books 1996), *Strategic Total Quality Management* (Quorum Books 1995). Dr. Madu is currently editing *the Handbook of Environmentally Conscious Manufacturing* (Kluwer Academic Publishers). Dr. Madu served as the editor-in-chief of the *International Journal of Quality Science* and is currently, the co-editor of the *International Journal of Quality and Reliability Management.* He also serves on the editorial board of several journals including *Computers & Operations Research, Engineering Management Journal,* and *Benchmarking International Journal.* He has also served as a consultant to several companies including ConEdison and International Bottled Water Association (IBWA). Dr. Madu can be reached through his email address at chrismadu@aol.com.

Chapter 1

1.0 HISTORY AND DEFINITION OF QUALITY FUNCTION DEPLOYMENT

The American Supplier Institute defines quality Function Deployment (QFD), 1989 as "a system for translating consumer requirements into appropriate company requirements at each stage from research and development to engineering and manufacturing to marketing/sales and distribution." Simply, QFD involves listening to the "voice of the customer" and systematically, translating the customer's requirements through each phase of the product development stage as requirements that the product must meet. It shifts away emphasis from meeting management and engineering demands in product development to that of meeting customers demands. Customer requirements are translated into requirements that must be met to deliver quality product or service to the customer. Listening to the "voice of the customer" starts from the product development stage and it is deployed throughout the firm. The focus of QFD is to maximize resources and minimize waste. QFD is therefore, a planning tool for developing new products and improving existing product [11]. Other definitions of QFD are offered as follows: Akao [1990] defined QFD as "a method for developing a design quality aimed at satisfying the consumer and then translating the consumer's demand into design targets and major quality assurance points to be used throughout the production phase." Thus, QFD assures that quality is designed into the product. By doing this, a considerable reduction in product development time is achieved. Sullivan [1986] defined QFD as "the main objective of any manufacturing company to bring new (and carryover) products to market sooner than the competition with lower cost and improved quality." He went on to emphasize that this concept involves the translation of customer requirements to appropriate technical

1

requirements for each stage of the product development and production. This process involves the marketing strategies, planning, product design and engineering, prototype evaluation, production process development, production and sales. Apparent from this definition is the fact that QFD applies also to existing products and services. Furthermore, QFD involves the entire product life cycle as well as the entire functional units of a business process. It leads to designing quality into the product by designing customer requirements into the product. More importantly, it significantly leads to a reduction in product development and introduction to the market place. Another objective of QFD is the optimal utilization of resources by ensuring that the product demanded by customers is produced correctly the first time and ensuring its introduction on a timely fashion.

QFD offers new challenges to businesses. It involves the entire "value supply chain" of the organization. It is important to evaluate each product development stage to see how it aligns with customer's requirements and the resources of the firm. This will therefore, lead to new set of standards and targets not only for engineers involved with product design but also for production workers at the floor level and suppliers. Thus, the entire supply chain is influenced by the "voice of the customer."

Clearly, listening to the "voice of the customer" and translating customer requirements into achievable targets to improve product quality is not easy. There will be some conflicting requirements. The customer may identify requirements that are not attainable at the same level, for example, the need to manufacture the best copy paper and also, protect the environment. These two are contradictory since the "best quality copy paper" will rely on 100 % virgin pulp which may conflict with the desire to protect the forestry. However, a copy paper that uses a mixture of virgin pulp and recycled pulp could be produced to balance this tradeoff. QFD, attempts to resolve such conflicts by focusing on the most important requirements. Furthermore, customer needs have to be balanced with design requirements and specifications. Some of the customer needs may not be attainable or feasible due to limitations in technology or available resources. Thus, customer needs, which are often referred to, as "whats" should be balanced with design requirements, referred to as "hows." The translation of "whats" into "hows" could be difficult and complex, as these can be interdependent and therefore, negatively correlated to each other. This may present another source of conflict that will also need to be resolved.

We have focused to this point on meeting customer requirements through QFD. There are many ways to solicit customer requirements. Notably, these requirements could be gathered through various market research methods such as customer survey questionnaires, interviews, focus groups, telephone surveys. A list of customer requirements is generated through this process and is referred to as "spoken" quality demands and performance expectations. However, there may be some product attributes that are assumed by the customer or the customer may not be aware of but may add to the value of the product. Such attributes should also be included and are referred to as "unspoken" attributes. Thus, the aim is not just to meet the requirements as specified or identified by the customer but also to go beyond and add as much features as possible and feasible to make the product the best in its class.

1.2   Brief history of QFD

The origins of QFD can be traced to Mitsubishi's Heavy Industries Kobe shipyard in Japan in the late 1960s where QFD was used to facilitate cross-functional product development process [5]. A 1986 survey by the Japanese Union of Scientists and Engineers (JUSE) showed that more than half of the companies surveyed was using QFD.   The application of QFD is pervasive in many of the manufacturing and service sectors in Japan. Toyota Motor Company and its suppliers are also among the major companies that have applied QFD in Japan. It is reported that Toyota auto body achieved a 60 % reduction in start-up costs for its new car model launch as a result of QFD application. Although pre-production cost went up slightly, other major costs were slashed by about 80 %. US manufacturers were however, slow in applying QFD. Its first major applications were in the automotive and electronic industries.

QFD is known by several names. As Emmanuel and Kroll [4] note, the original name for QFD in Japan is *hin shitsu, ki nou, ten kai*. There are several translations for these words including "features mechanization evolution, qualities function diffusion, or quality function deployment." The problem here is in the direct translation of the original Japanese words to English language. Other popular names used for QFD include Policy Deployment, Voice of the Customer,

4 *Chapter 1*

House of Quality, Customer-Driven Engineering, and Matrix Product Planning.

1.3 Motivation for QFD

Undoubtedly, the increased competition in both the US and global markets helped to focus the attention of US businesses on the application of QFD. As Emmanuel and Kroll [4] note, the QFD as a planning tool, reached the US during the quality revolution of the 1980s. Japanese companies were gradually taking over many of the businesses that US manufacturers once dominated. There was a significant interest by top management to understand Japanese management practices especially as they relate to product quality. Major companies in the US embarked on studying these new quality philosophies that were coming out from Japan. Furthermore, they understood that in order to compete effectively, they must realign their strategies and develop plans like their Japanese counterparts that focus on achieving customer satisfaction. QFD became one of the important tools that could help them understand the customer and integrate the customer's requirements into the design and production of goods and services. By doing so, they will be able to regain lost markets and compete effectively. The incentive for survival in today's business was therefore, a motivating force in the adoption of these new practices by American businesses.

Hales and David [1995] note that product failures could be devastating to a company and may drain both the human and financial resources. They point out that some companies that maintain volumes of information pertaining to the customer and state-of-the art design and manufacturing tools have witnessed high-profile flops. For example, products such as new Coke, dry beer, and smokeless cigarettes. Therefore, the emphasis with QFD is not merely to collect volumes of information on customer requirements but to be able to develop a structured and systematic approach when analyzing such information and translate its results to the design and manufacture of customer-driven products. They note that sometimes, products or services that customers do not want manifest themselves in terms of "functionality, practicality, quality, cost, timing" etc. They advocate the use of QFD with target costing to get a company to be customer-focused. QFD emphasizes the fact that the product can be designed and produced to meet the customer requirements. However, cost should be a consideration in determining what the market could bear.

1.4   Benefits of QFD

QFD has many demonstrable benefits especially for firms interested in achieving competitiveness, increasing market share, improving productivity and improving the bottom line. Those companies that have adopted QFD have reported significant cost reductions. How these gains are achieved are outlined below:

- Reduction in cycle time is achieved. The product is introduced to the market faster. Start-up costs are lower. Quality is improved. There is a reduction in number of engineering changes that may be required.
- Products are produced at a lower cost due to the reduction in operational cost.
- QFD is normally applied in a cross-functional team context. For example, members from the different functional areas of the firm organize to develop new product concepts. Members of the cross-functional team have diverse backgrounds and are able to share common information and understand each other's views. This process of sharing information and listening to each other, helps resolve potential conflicts and assures that organizational goals are not suboptimized. Members begin to develop a more holistic picture of the problem. Information gathered from the different functional teams can also be shared. For example, marketing, sales and distribution departments often have more contact with customers. They are able to relay information obtained through this process to those in engineering that will have to incorporate such considerations during product design and development.
- Information gathering is an ongoing process in the use of QFD. It is important to maintain a database of customer requirements that may be gathered from different sources. This information could be used repeatedly to design new product or improve existing products.
- Design and production efficiency is achieved through QFD. Members of the cross-functional teams develop a critical analysis of their functions and ensure that customer requirements are integrated at every phase of product development. This will ensure that products are designed and produced right the first time, thus

reducing the cost of production, minimizing waste, and maximizing efficiency.

- Organizational harmony may foster through formation of cross-functional teams. The functional units will no longer be competing against each other rather, they will be working towards a common goal. Such teams, foster increased openness and sharing of information with the ultimate goal of designing and producing products that will lead to high customer satisfaction.
- Problems are easier to identify by listening to the "voice of the customer." These problems can be corrected to achieve successful introduction of the product in the market place. Also, the decision making process may include significant customer groups in the team to help ensure that the products are designed and produced with the customer in mind.
- Market information gained through QFD can be used to determine product price, quality, and functionality.
- Product development is customer-driven and supports value-engineering analysis in order to cut cost and add value to the product.
- Bottom line is improved through the application of QFD. Some of the reported influence on bottom line are as follows:
- High market acceptance of the product
- Reduction in design cycle time
- Increased competitiveness
- Reduction in design changes
- Reduction in production cost
- Improved efficiency.
- Improved worker morale.

1.5 Conclusion

In summary, QFD is a planning tool that can help businesses plan product design and production with increased efficiency. Its aim is to ensure that customer requirements are integrated in the design and production of the product. By doing so, a product that meets high quality standards as defined by the customer can be produced. This ensures that the product is not offered to the customer as seen by the design engineer but rather as seen by the customer itself. If the customer's requirements are effectively considered, then it is likely that the customer will accept the final product. This will help improve the competitiveness of the manufacturer, ensure customer loyalty, reduce waste, and improve the bottom line. The next chapter will focus on the "voice of the customer."

References

1. Akao, Y., Quality Function Deployment, Cambridge, MA: Productivity Press, 1990.
2. American Supplier Institute (1989) Quality Function Deployment Implementation Manual, American Supplier Institute, Dearborn, MI.
3. Day, R. G., Quality Function Deployment – Linking a Company with its Customers, Milwaukee, WI: ASQC Quality Press, 1993.
4. Emmanuel, J.T., and Kroll, D.E., "Concurrent Engineering," in Handbook of Total Quality Management, Boston, MA: Kluwer Academic Publishers, 1998 (ed., Madu, C.N.)
5. Eseteghalian, A., Verma, B., Foutz, T., and Thompson, S., "Customer focused approach to design: new methodologies consider environmental impact on product development," *Engineering & Technology for a Sustainable World*, 06-01-98, pp 7(2).
6. Evans, J.R., and Lindsay, W.M., The Management & Control of Quality, 4th edition, Cincinnati, OH: South-Western Publishing, 1999.
7. Gale, B. T., and Wood, R.C., Managing Customer Value-Creating Quality and Service that Customers Can See, NY: The Free Press, 1994.
8. Hales, R., and Staley, D., "Mix target costing, QFD for successful new products," *Marketing News*, Jan. 2, 1995, 22(1), pp. 18-20.
9. Mears, P., Quality Improvement Tools & Techniques, NY: McGraw Hill Inc., 1995.
10. Sullivan, L. P., "Quality Function Deployment," *Quality Progress*, June 1986.
11. Vonderembse, M.A., and Van Fossen, T., "Quality Function Deployment," in Handbook of Total Quality Management, Boston, MA: Kluwer Academic Publishers, 1998 (ed., Madu, C.N.).

Chapter 2

2.0 VOICE OF THE CUSTOMER

Quality function deployment (QFD) is a process of listening to the "voice of the customer," identifying the customer's needs, and incorporating those needs in the design and production of goods and services. We noted in chapter 1 that this process involves the entire supply chain with the goal of producing the goods or services that the customer actually wants and adding value to those goods and services. Listening to the "voice of the customer" ensures the manufacturer or service provider that features the customer wants is included in the product or service. The key fact however, is listening to the "voice of the customer" and identifying customer requirements as articulated by the customer. The aim of this chapter is to specifically outline how manufacturers can make effective use of this learning process.

There are three levels in listening to the "voice of the customer." The first level involves an understanding of the basic wants and needs of the customer. This involves the use of experimental techniques to identify customer requirements. Experimental approaches to be taken here include the use of field surveys, focus groups, questionnaires, to identify a list of requirements that are "important" to the customer. These requirements must be translated into measurable operational forms. For example, a homeowner's requirement to a builder that the house be well built is vague and does not identify what features will make the house well built. Therefore, the request needs to be broken down to specific points such as: the foundation should be supported by adequate pillars, the electric outlets work, the trims are in place, the doors close properly, the walls are smooth, the ceilings are high, etc. In other words, vague statements by customers must be broken down to operational forms. These as we stated earlier are the "spoken" quality attributes that must be present in the home. However, there are other "unspoken" attributes that the builder must include. For example, what effect will extreme weather conditions have on the house? Is the house accident proof? Thus, both the "spoken" and "unspoken" customer requirements must be present if the "voice of the customer" is to be heard.

The second phase involves the extension of the product design beyond these "spoken" and "unspoken" customer requirements. There are some customers' requirements that are not apparent from the first phase that designers should be aware of. Designers need to scrutinise how and why customers use their product [5]. Alternative ways should be offered to cover this range of applications and usage by customers. For example, consider a college in a metropolitan area that attracts adult students. These students may be primarily interested in quality education but may also be interested in the convenience of getting higher education. There is a variety of ways that the college could provide this service to its student population. One way may be to offer evening programs. Another way may be to offer weekend classes. Other more technologically advanced forms may be to offer lectures through video-conferencing at their job sites, or lectures through the Internet. By doing this, QFD drives the company by forcing the design team to identify hidden customer requirements and offering ways to satisfy such requirements.

Third, there are many features of the product that the customer may be unaware of. However, the cross-functional team that work on the QFD can identify these features and point them out to the customer. Customers are often unaware of advances in technology and research that could help improve the quality of the product. For example, with the growing focus on sustainable development, a manufacturer may identify new ways to minimise waste or use less energy in product design and production. This may increase customer satisfaction and help the manufacturer expand its market share. The manufacturer can increase customer satisfaction by trying to understand the customer beyond the horizon of the product and determining what is important to the customer. It is important to understand the customer's behavior and how that may affect some of his actions. For example, a customer interested in buying a new car, may identify operational features such as aesthetics, dependability, and availability of service as features of interest to her. However, the same customer may be interested in cars that burn cleaner and consume less gas. Safety issues may also be important and the customer may prefer cars that offer a combination of product features as well as these other important attributes.

2.1   Formation of Cross-Functional Teams

Cross-functional teams are used in most QFD projects. The team will comprise of representatives from the different functional departments or units that are either directly or indirectly affected by the project. In a business organisation, this team could include representatives from engineering, marketing, production, and finance. The objective or the goal of the team will be to find an efficient method to address customer needs or requirements in the design, production and delivery of products and services. Thus, this team must address the feasibility of using the organisation's resources to satisfy customer requirements. The use of cross-functional teams also has other important benefits to the organisation as follows:

- It ensures that all the related functional units are committed to the project. When members of these teams participate in the project, they are committed to the successful completion of the project.
- Organisations use their resources more efficiently if the various functional units work towards a common goal. The use of cross-functional teams exposes members of the team to the need for achieving organisational goals and help reduce internal competition. Therefore, marketing will not see its goals as different from that of engineering. The different units will come to understand the purpose of the organisation as that of satisfying customer requirements in a more efficient way. And, once that is achieved, customer satisfaction will also be attained and the business will thrive.
- The use of teams enables information sharing. For example, product designers come to learn from marketing how the customer perceives certain aspects of the product. Designers come to learn from finance about the financial viability or feasibility of certain projects. Through teams, information flows laterally and can be used timely for effective decision making.
- Customers are the major beneficiaries of cross-functional team activities. The different functional groups have different worldviews, which helps broaden each participant's scope and view. These different perspectives could be instrumental in designing products that appeal to a wider range of consumer groups.
- Members in cross-functional teams are empowered. They feel the responsibility to make decisions and take corrective actions. This will help increase their organisational commitment and also, helps

reduce organisational waste. Morale and motivation may also improve.
- Through cross-functional teams, brainstorming sessions can be held to generate ideas for product improvement and development.

Although cross-functional teams are heralded as useful in designing and producing high quality products, however, such teams could become counter-productive if not well implemented. Some of the problems that may arise are as follows:
- Group-think mentality can often emerge from any team. This happens when members perceive domination of the team by one or few individuals. So, rather than team members actively participating and contributing their ideas, they become subjected to accept the view of one or more dominant members of the group. This has to be avoided if customer requirements are to be satisfied.
- Feeling of alienation may emerge. This again, is related to the group-think mentality. This happens when members feel that they have no role to play other than to rubber stamp pre-conceived ideas.
- Conflicts may often arise. However, it is important to productively resolve any conflicts and avoid formation of interest groups within the cross-functional groups. Formation of conflicting sub-groups will invariably lead to sub-optimisation.

It is important for members of cross-functional teams to have an open mind about the problem to be solved and work towards a common goal – that of the organisation's success by improving customer satisfaction. This can be achieved by focusing on what is important to the customer and how the organisation can satisfy the customer using its resources.

2.2   Identifying Customer Requirements

The entire premise of QFD rests on identifying and satisfying customer requirements. Although many QFD research have presented examples of customer requirements and how they have been matched with design requirements, few have really discussed in detail how customer requirements are identified. Granted, many have mentioned techniques such as the use of focus groups, marketing information, etc., it is important to have a systematic way to identify customer requirements. Customer requirement forms the foundation of QFD. If the wrong requirements are identified, the product designed to meet such requirements will lose its appeal and will therefore, fail. The "identification of customer requirements" is the most critical step in developing a QFD. We shall examine two popular methods to identify customer requirements. These methods focus mostly on identifying the "spoken requirements" of the customer. Hayes [2] refers to the first method as "quality dimension development approach." Flanagan [1954] developed the second method and it is known as the "critical incident approach".

2.3 Quality Dimension Development

The use of the term "quality dimension" is synonymous to the term "customer requirements." Customer requirements specifically represent the attributes or features of a product or service that the customer deems important in achieving his or her customer satisfaction. Clearly, a customer can perceive several attributes and these attributes may differ from product to product and from service to service. However, certain industries have universal attributes. For example, in the auto industry, attributes such as safety are always important to the customer. In the service sector for example, Kennedy and Young [1989] identified four common attributes or quality dimension as availability, responsiveness, convenience, and timeliness. Authors of SERVQUAL model present five dimensions of service quality as tangibles, reliability, responsiveness, assurance, and empathy [4]. These quality dimensions are however, specific to service organisations. Through extensive literature reviews, members of the cross-functional teams for QFD can identify specific quality dimensions for their particular industries. However, such dimensions of quality may not cover all the important attributes or customer requirements for a specific product. It is therefore, important to go beyond the "generic industry attributes" to identify specifically the attributes of the product that the customer needs. Thus, there is a need for the cross-functional team to conduct a detailed study of the product or service to identify other hidden attributes. Such studies employ knowledgeable experts and focus customer groups who understand the product and are able to offer insights on the customer's expectations of the product. Through this, a list of quality attributes can be identified. It is important also, to conduct benchmarking analysis to identify other attributes present in competitor's products. The attributes identified have to be clearly stated to avoid ambiguities. For example, important consumer research publications that do a comparative analysis of products could be an important source of information since such publications often compare similar products by looking at quality attributes that are important to customers.

The quality dimension approach relies heavily on the cross-functional teams as experts who know and understand the product's purpose or function. Such teams could therefore, breakdown the product into its functional components and study and analyse it to see how the needs of the customer are satisfied. Suppose we take an auto manufacturer as an example, a sample of customer requirement issues may include the following:

Operational: The ease of opening the car door

Operational: The length of time or mileage between scheduled service.

Aesthetics: The size or shape of the car

Availability of Support: The ease to which service can be obtained

Responsiveness: The time it takes to perform scheduled service

These attributes can be grouped into keywords or dimensions of quality and each evaluated to eliminate redundancies. The cross-functional team can now work with specific quality dimensions that cover a range of customer requirement issues. In addition to these attributes which we have referred to in chapter 1 as the "spoken requirements," there are "unspoken requirements" that the members of the cross-functional teams must also identify and ensure that they are present in the product. For example, certain levels of safety should be guaranteed; the car should meet emission laws; the car must have an aesthetic appeal; the price should be reasonable; etc. Thus, both "spoken" and "unspoken" requirements should be present.

When a long list of attributes is generated, it is possible that some of the attributes may not be important or may add little or no value to the product. Rather than the team wasting valuable resources to tackle insignificant problems, it is important that some method be devised to assign priorities to the customer requirements that have been identified. The focus should be on solving the critical and important problems. It is more important to include the major customer requirements in a satisfying manner to the customer than to marginally consider every conceivable factor. We shall now discuss the critical incident approach.

2.4   Critical Incident Approach

Flanagan [1954] developed this approach. It could be used to develop customer satisfaction questionnaires to understand customer requirements. This method views organisational performance from the perspective of the customer. The customer views organisational performance from the aspects of the organisation it is directly in contact with. With respect to manufacturing, the customer is in direct contact with the product. And, with respect to service, the customer is in direct contact with the staff. The customer looks at the product or service attribute on how the attribute may positively or negatively affect organisational performance. An attribute that will have a negative effect would impact on the customer's positive perception of the organisation thereby, negatively affecting the customer's perception of organisational performance. However, an attribute that has a positive impact will be more desirable to the customer. Critical incidents are therefore, the "quality attributes" of the organisation that the customer is directly in contact with. These critical incidents could be obtained either through individual or group interviewing. This process is conducted by dealing directly with people who have used the product or service and are in a position to offer specific judgements on the different attributes of the product or service. It is recommended that between 10 to 20 customers be interviewed and each customer should be asked to describe 5 to 10 positive and negative instances for the product or service respectively [2]. In addition, the questions should be specific and avoid the use of general terms. This should help the customer to focus on specifics. The use of a large number of customers helps to reduce the possibility of obtaining incomplete information. For example, information not obtained from one interviewee can be compensated from subsequent interviews with other customers. From the interviewing process, a list of critical incidents could be developed which can be grouped again into specific "quality attributes."

2.5 Analysis of quality attributes

It is important to solve the critical problem. A major problem that may arise from using these techniques to solicit customer requirements is that a long list may be generated that may be unmanageable. Our recommendation will be to identify both the "spoken" and "unspoken" product or service attributes through these methods. Organise the attributes in to quality dimensions and develop a "customer satisfaction survey" to relate these quality attributes to the specific product or service. The aim should be to identify from a more typical group which customer requirements are important. The survey should be administered to a random sample of existing and potential customers. The survey should be analysed statistically to identify which quality attributes are significant or important in achieving customer satisfaction. This will help to narrow down the list of "critical incidents" to quality attributes that a typical group of the customer base views as important. The cross-functional team can then focus its effort in satisfying those significant requirements. This approach will help the cross-functional team address the most important customer requirement issues, save time, and optimise the use of limited resources.

2.6   Conclusion

In this chapter, we have discussed issues relating to the "voice of the customer." We discussed the formation of cross-functional teams to identify customer requirements from a product or service. In addition, we noted potential benefits and problems with the use of cross-functional teams and the need to focus on overall organisational goals. We note the two important methods to identify customer requirements namely: quality dimension development and critical incident approach. We conclude by emphasising the use of questionnaire surveys administered to a random sample of customers to identify significant customer requirement issues. This will help the cross-functional QFD team to focus on the most important customer requirement issues, better utilise its resources, and timely design and produce the product and service needed by its customers.

Reference

1. Flanagan, M., "The critical incident technique," Psychological Bulletin 51: 327-358, 1954.
2. Hayes, B.E., Measuring customer satisfaction: Development and use of questionnaires, Milwauke, Wis.: ASQC Quality Press, 1992.
3. Kennedy, D.A., and Young, B.J., "Managing quality in staff areas," Quality Progress 22 (10), 87-91.
4. Parasuraman, A., Zeithaml, V.A., and Berry, L.L., "SERVQUAL: A multiple-item scale for measuring customer perceptions of service quality," Journal of Retailing 64: 12-40, 1988.
5. Vonderembse, M.A., and Van Fossen, T., "Quality Function Deployment," in Handbook of Total Quality Management, Boston, MA: Kluwer Academic Publishers, 1998 (ed., Madu, C.N.)

Chapter 3

3.0 HOUSE OF QUALITY

In this chapter, we discuss how to build the 'House of Quality.' In chapter 2, we discussed how product or service characteristics that are important to the customer can be identified. However, these product characteristics must be integrated into the design of the product. Charts are important in building the 'House of Quality.' By using charts or diagrams, information obtained by listening to the 'voice of the customer' can be summarized and compared to design requirements. The 'House of Quality' is therefore, a blueprint for product development. We shall breakdown in a stepwise form, how the 'House of Quality' can be built.

Step 1: In chapter 2, we identified customer requirements. We also noted that this could be an extensive list and it is important to identify the significant requirements and eliminate any redundancies that may exist. A list of the important customer requirements should be constructed and should include product or service attributes as identified by customers. This list is often referred to as 'whats' to signify what the customer actually wants to see in a product or service. However, care must be taken to ensure that these 'whats' can be made operational. For example, consider the subscription to an Internet Online Service. It is not enough for a customer to state that he or she needs a 'reliable or good online service.' The term 'reliable or good' is broad and should be broken down to attributes that could be used to define such an adjective. For example, a good online service provider may have the following attributes: local access numbers, support for a wide range of modems, accessible online and telephone help, easy access to Internet, ease of access to the server, etc. Thus, the 'whats' of a customer has to be broken down to primary, secondary, and tertiary levels of information. It is apparent that the primary objective in this example is to have a good or reliable online

17

server. However, the attributes used to qualify the adjective "good" are secondary and must be present to achieve the primary objective. These secondary objectives can be further broken down to tertiary levels of information. For example, 'ease of access to the server' may include offering several local access numbers that the user can dial up if one is busy. The list of 'whats' as identified by the customer should be clearly defined.

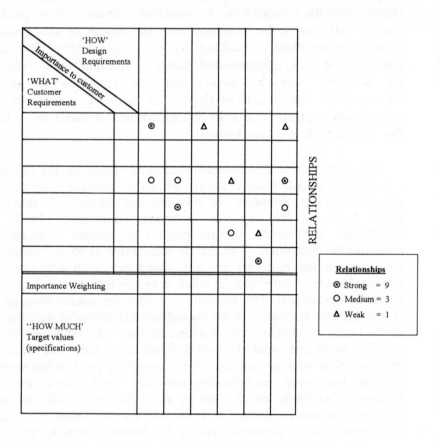

Figure 3.1: QFD Relationship Matrix

Step 2: Once this list of 'whats' is clarified, a list of the design requirements known as the 'hows' should be developed. This list of 'hows' shows how design requirements can influence the attainment of 'whats' as identified by the customer. The design characteristics are often under the control of the manufacturer or the producer and are at times, referred to as 'engineering characteristics.' They could be expressed in technical terms within the organisation and are measurable. For example, what is the maximum transfer rate of information that the server provides (i.e., 56kbs). This could partly measure the ease of access to the Internet or World Wide Web. This step involves the translation of customer requirements to design requirements. This process is compounded by the fact that there may exist interdependent relationships between customer requirements and design requirements. In other words, some of the customer requirements may conflict with design requirements or rather, the 'whats' and 'hows' may negatively influence one another. However, this is to be expected because there are multiple goals identified in the 'whats' and in trying to achieve all these goals, there will be some tradeoffs. If such conflicts do not exist, it is possible that an error has been committed. A well-designed product or service is likely to involve tradeoffs (American Supplier Institute, 1989). Potential conflicts that are identified must be resolved productively. With the use of QFD, such conflicts can be effectively resolved during the product design stage thereby, reducing the need for significant engineering changes downstream.

Step 3: Steps 1 and 2 form the basis for the first QFD chart (Figure 3-1). Figure 3-1 has several components. First, this figure must contains the list of significant customer requirements (whats) shown on the left side of the matrix as rows and a list of design requirements (hows) listed in columns near the top. A definition is given on the top left side of the relationship symbols used to show the relationship between a customer requirement and a design requirement. For example, a Δ symbol shown at an intersection point between customer requirement and design requirement means the weakest design requirement to satisfy that customer requirement. This figure also contains a column titled 'importance to customer.' This column denotes the relative importance of the customer requirement attributes to the customer. This will help designers focus more attention on achieving those attributes that are of utmost importance to the customer. The figure also has at the bottom, the 'target values or specifications or how much.' And a row that contains the importance weighting. The importance weighting at the bottom is similar to the 'importance to customer' column. This denotes the importance for the different design requirements. The target values are the specifications that could be achieved through engineering design. For example, suppose that one customer requirement in a new car is the "ease to close the car door." A design requirement may be to investigate the "energy requirement to close the door," and the target specification may be to reduce energy level to 7.5ft/lb (Hauser and Clausing 1988). Thus, the target values deals with the 'how much' or specifics. The QFD cross-functional team generates these values, as they believe them to satisfy customer requirements. Design requirements must be compared to measurable targets that are under the control of the designer.

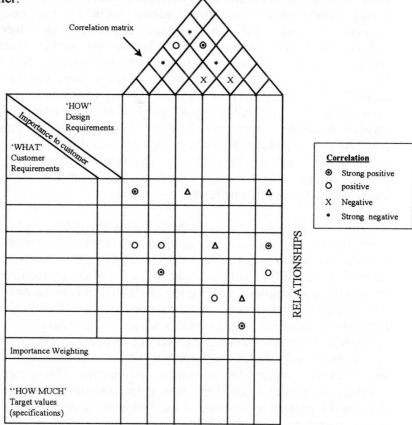

Figure 3.2: QFD Relationship and Correlation Matrix

Step 4: Figure 3-2 is used to illustrate this step. This involves the addition of the correlation matrix to actually form a 'house' or rather, the house of quality. This correlation matrix shows the correlation between the different design requirements. On the right side figure 3-2 is the definition of the symbols used for the correlation. For example, the use of the symbol * denotes strong negative correlation between two design requirements and X denotes negative correlation. Of utmost importance is the negative and strong negative correlation observed between the design requirements. Such relationships imply that there is a conflict in trying to achieve both requirements jointly. Thus as one is being achieved, the other is being compromised. This conflict needs to be resolved or a trade-off decision has to be made. Such decision could involve retaining the design requirement that has the higher importance weighting.

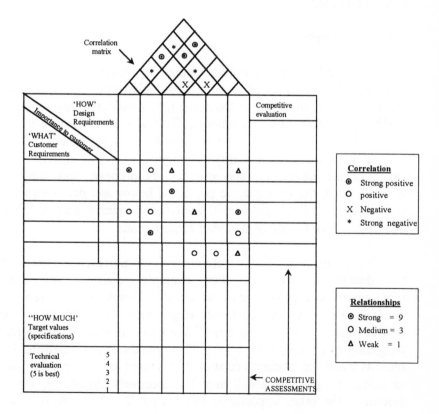

Figure 3.3: House of Quality

Step 5: Figure 3-3 is a modification of figure 3-2 to include two new components namely "competitive evaluation" and "technical evaluation." These two offer a benchmarking of the manufacturer's product or service to that of competitors in several ways. For example, with the competitive evaluation, the manufacturer is compared to its competitors on each of the customer requirements identified by the customer. Similarly, for the technical evaluation, the manufacturer is compared against its competitors based on the design requirements to satisfy customer requirements. One thing not shown yet in this diagram is that the manufacturer is positioned in a scale against its competitors. Ideally, the manufacturer will like to out perform its competitors. Thus, the manufacturer has to make the effort to be the best in class. To put all these in perspective, we shall illustrate with an example. Figure 3.4 is adapted from the case presented by Hauser and Clausing [1988].

A Case Example

We shall adapt the example presented by Hauser and Clausing. In that example, they showed that for a particular product, series of sub-charts could be created. For example, they considered developing the QFD for the door of an automobile. This alone will require its own QFD chart, which eventually could be tied in with the other QFDs that may be needed to build a quality automobile. Customer attributes for a car door are developed and grouped as primary, secondary and tertiary. Thus, the example we presented below and demonstrated in other sections of this book will focus on designing and building a quality car door to satisfy customer requirements.

Using figure 3-4, we can determine the importance weighting for the design requirements. For example, consider the design requirement "energy needed to close door." This design requirement is strongly related to the customer requirement "easy to close" and medium related to "easy to open." We can determine its importance weighting as $(7 \times 9) + (3 \times 3) = 72$ where the strong relationship is rated as 9 and the moderate relationship is rated as 3. The 'importance to customer' weights are 7 and 3 respectively. Similarly, we can determine the other importance weights as 72, 57, 43, 9, 6, and 45 respectively.

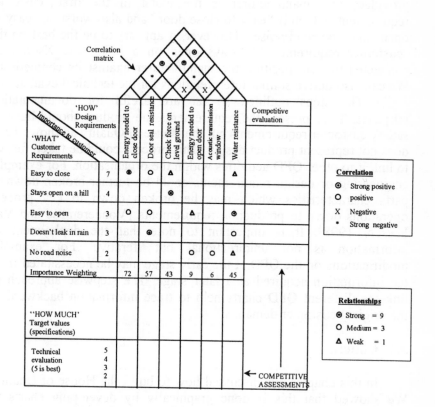

Figure 3.4: QFD Example

Thus, in terms of importance, we can order the design requirements as follows: energy needed to close door, door seal resistance, water resistance, check force on level ground, energy needed to open door, and acoustic transmission window. We also notice that there are some negative correlations. For example, energy needed to close door is strongly negatively correlated to energy needed to open door. Thus, this conflict has to be resolved or a trade-off has to be made. In terms of trade-off, it is seen from the importance weighting that the energy needed to close door is more important than the energy needed to open door. Similarly, this example shows that door seal resistance is positively correlated with water resistance.

The other important information that is gained here is the competitive assessment information. As seen from the information provided, this manufacturer is the worst in the first 'customer requirement' which is "easy to close door" and also worst on "easy to open" and "no road noise." However, it appears to be the best on the "customer requirement" "stays open on a hill." The Xs are all connected to help position the manufacturer against its competitors. We can also derive similar interpretations for the technical evaluation.

The steps outlined so far are useful for documentation purposes. They present the requirements the product should have to satisfy customer requirements but the House of Quality as shown here, does not represent product design. This process could be taken further to link it to other QFD activities within the organisation. For example, engineering or design requirements could be further broken down to parts characteristics which may be broken down to key process operations down to production requirements [Vonderembse and Van Fossen, 1998]. It is important to note that the deployment of information is not unidirectional but iterative. For example, modifications on the QFD at the early stage may be necessitated from the information acquired at a later stage. The stepwise approach to link the different QFD charts help to trace information backward to the original customer demands.

3.1 Conclusions

In this chapter, we discussed how to build the House of Quality. We showed that this is done graphically by developing charts to organise "customer requirements" and "engineering or design requirements" needed to satisfy the customer. We also showed by example how to interpret information from the QFD chart. We must caution however, that the example is for illustrative purposes only. Furthermore, different organisations may modify the QFD chart to better suit their needs. We also noted that QFD is an iterative process that requires linking each phase. The procedures are similar however and every stage may involve its own QFD chart. For example, their may be a need for a QFD chart for design requirements as they will be met by 'parts characteristics' and 'parts characteristics' as they will be satisfied by 'key process operations' and so on. By linking all these different QFD charts, it becomes easier to trace information back to their original sources. Although the final QFD charts may look complicated, they are not difficult to generate once the relevant information is available.

3.2 References

1. American Supplier Institute (1989) <u>Quality Function Deployment Implementation Manual</u>, American Supplier Institute, Dearborn, MI.
2. Hauser, J.R., and Clausing, D., "<u>The House of Quality,</u>" Harvard Business Review, May-June 1988, pp. 62-73.
3. Vonderembse, M.A., and Van Fossen, T., "<u>Quality Function Deployment,</u>" in <u>Handbook of Total Quality Management</u>, Boston, MA: Kluwer Academic Publishers, 1998 (ed., Madu, C.N.)

26

3.2 References

1. American Supplier Institute (1987), Quality Function Deployment Implementation Manual, American Supplier Institute, Dearborn, MI.

2. Hauser, J.R. and Clausing, D., "The House of Quality", Harvard Business Review, May-June 1988, pp. 62-73.

3. Vonderembse, M.A., and Van Fossen, T., "Quality Function Deployment," in Handbook of Total Quality Management, Boston, MA: Kluwer Academic Publishers, 1998 (ed. Madu, C.N.).

Chapter 4

4.0 QFD AND THE ANALYTIC HIERARCHY PROCESS (AHP)

Chapter 3 illustrates how to build the House of Quality. Apart from identifying customer requirements for a product or service and developing the list of design requirements to satisfy such needs, we noticed the QFD charts contain relative weights on the customer requirements. Also, the chart contains benchmarking information. In this chapter, we shall focus on the relative weights that are assigned to customer requirements.

The main purpose of assigning relative weights to the customer requirements is to make sure the customer's priorities are integrated in the product design. Obviously, these critical requirements are the ones that customers will frequently look for in the product or service. Once these important requirements are absent, the customer can not be satisfied. Clearly, there are several requirements that the customer may want present in a product. However, the manufacturer is operating with limited resources and may not be able to satisfy all these needs. It is therefore, important to focus on the most important needs of the customer. Furthermore, even when it may be possible to satisfy all the customer requirements, it is important to the manufacturer to identify the most critical needs of the customer. Due attention should be paid to ensure that such requirements are integrated in the product design.

In the example we presented in chapter 3 (Figure 3-4), we assigned weights to customer requirement items to show the importance of these items to the customer. For example, a weight of 7 was assigned to 'easy to close' while a weight of 2 was assigned to 'no road noise.' These weights show for example that 'easy to close' is more important to the customer than 'no road noise.' There are however, potential problems with this method of assignment. First, such assignment could become arbitrary if there is no structured approach to reach to these numbers. Second, with several customer requirements to consider at the same time, it may be difficult to arrive at a meaningful weight assignment. Third, it may be difficult to measure the consistency of the decision maker(s) that assigns these weights. Yet, as we saw from Figure 3-4, these weight assignments are critical in deriving useful information from the QFD chart. For example, the importance weighting obtained for the design requirements are influenced by the 'importance to customer' weights that were used. Thus, if these weights are inaccurately assigned, the organisation will focus on the insignificant design requirements and will therefore, design products that may not meet customer requirements.

What we intend to do is present a structured approach to assign the 'importance to customer' weights. These weights will then be validated in terms of their consistency. The process used for this purpose is known as the "Analytic Hierarchy Process" or AHP for short.

Briefly, the AHP is "a multi-criteria decision model that uses hierarchic or network structure to represent a decision problem and then develops priorities for alternatives based on the decision maker's judgment throughout the system" [Saaty p. 157]. Figure 4-1 that depicts a network of customer requirements is an example. Here, the goal is to determine the relative importance of these customer requirement items to the customer.

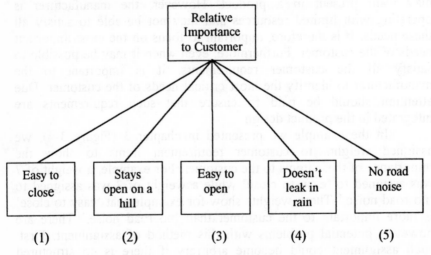

Figure 4-1: Customer requirement importance rating

The AHP has been used in many decision-making contexts and it is quite applicable for QFD application for the following reasons:

1. The AHP is based on pairwise comparison between competing alternatives. For example, each QFD team member can take only a pair of customer requirements and compare at a time (i.e., 'easy to close' compared to 'stays open on a hill' in terms of their relative importance to the customer). This pairwise comparison reduces the number of customer requirement items that each member has to consider at any one time to be able to assign a relative importance weight.

2. It allows for the consideration of both objective (i.e., the price of a product) and subjective (i.e., customer's perception of a product characteristic) factors.

3. The consistency in the judgement of the QFD team members could be easily derived and the quality of their judgement can be evaluated. Although consistency does not infer quality decisions, however, all quality decisions are consistent. When the QFD team members' judgements are consistent, there will be a greater likelihood that quality decisions will be reached. In other words, it will be more likely that the weight assigned to customer requirements may reflect the importance of these requirements to the customer.

4. As we alluded in Chapters 1 and 2, QFD team is comprised of cross-functional departments. Clearly, with multiple people involved in the decision making process, it becomes much harder to obtain a single number that will denote their agreed importance weight to a customer requirement item. It is better that each member assigns his or her own weight independently to avoid the weights being 'biased' from 'group-think' syndrome. The AHP allows each member to independently assign weights to the customer requirements and then, these weights are combined to arrive at a group index.

5. Conflict resolution is an important part of QFD. We noted in the case of design requirements where there might be a need for trade-off. However, conflict may be as a result of the significance of some of the customer requirement items. Such conflicts can easily be identified through AHP [1] and other management techniques could be used jointly with AHP to resolve such conflicts.

We shall now, apply the AHP to the same problem we covered in chapter 3 and shown as Figure 3-4. Table 1 illustrates a pairwise comparison matrix for the customer requirements. The customer requirements are codified as 1 = easy to close; 2 = stays open on a hill;

3 = easy to open; 4 = doesn't leak in rain; and 5 = no road noise. Thus, when an item is compared to itself, its relative importance over itself is 1. When however, easy to close (1) is compared to easy to open (3), the relative importance of (1) over (3) is 7 which means that "easy to close" has very strong importance over "easy to open." Each QFD team member conducts his or her own pairwise comparison of the customer requirement items. The QFD team assignment is obtained by taking a geometric mean of all team members' assignment for each pair of comparison. The weighting scale used in AHP are defined as follows: 1 = equal importance; 3 = moderate importance of one customer requirement item over the other; 5 = strong importance; 7 = very strong importance; and 9 = extreme importance. The even numbers 2, 4, 6, and 8 are used for compromise, while reciprocals are used to show inverse comparisons.

	1	2	3	4	5
1	1.000000	5.000000	7.000000	7.000000	9.000000
2	0.200000	1.000000	5.000000	7.000000	7.000000
3	0.142857	0.200000	1.000000	1.000000	3.000000
4	0.142857	0.142857	1.000000	1.000000	3.000000
5	0.111111	0.142857	0.333333	0.333333	1.000000
Column Total	1.596825	6.485714	14.333333	16.333333	23.000000

Table 4.1: Pairwise Comparison of Customer Requirements

Thus, from Table 1, we see that 'easy to close' has a strong importance over 'stays open on a hill.' Since we have made this assignment, we see that when 'stays open on a hill' (2 on the row) is compared to 'easy to close' (1 on the column), we simply put the inverse of the original comparison in that cell. That inverse is 1/5 as shown in Table 1.

Once we have created this pairwise matrix of comparison of customer requirements, we are ready to apply the method of the AHP. The steps to follow are as follows:

Step 1:
Obtain the column total. This is done by obtaining the sum of all the weights in each cell in a particular column. For example, for column 1, the sum is 1.596825 and for column 5, the sum is 23.

	1	2	3	4	5	Row Average
1	0.62624	0.77093	0.48837	0.42857	0.39130	0.541083
2	0.12525	0.15419	0.34884	0.42857	0.30435	0.272238
3	0.08946	0.03084	0.06977	0.06122	0.13044	0.076345
4	0.08946	0.02203	0.06977	0.06122	0.13044	0.074583
5	0.06958	0.02203	0.02326	0.02041	0.04348	0.03575
						1

Table 4.2: Row Average Operation

Step 2:
Divide each entry in a cell by its column total. For example, the column total for "easy to close" is 1.596825. When the first entry in that column which is 1 is divided by the column total of 1.596825, the value of 0.626243 shown in Table 4.2 is obtained.

Step 3:
Obtain the row averages. These row averages are known as the priority indices. For example, the row average of 0.541 shows the relative importance of the customer requirement 'easy to open'. It is seen here that 'easy to open' is the most important customer requirement item followed by 'stays open on a hill' with a priority index of 0.272. The least important customer requirement item is 'no road noise' with a priority index of 0.035. It appears that 'easy to open' and 'doesn't leak in rain' are of equal importance with priority indexes of 0.076 and 0.074 respectively. Thus, the QFD team should focus more attention in satisfying the customer by designing the product for 'easy to close' and 'stays open on hill,' while the other items are of less significance.

Step 4:
However, before these priority indexes can be used in a QFD framework, it is important to validate them by checking for consistency in the judgement of the QFD team. This is done by using the priority indexes generated in Table 4.3 and the original weight assignments in Table 4.1. Each column of Table 1 is multiplied by its corresponding priority index given as the rows of Table 3. These products are then summed. As shown in this example, the sum is 5.400637. This operation is provided below:

	1	2	3	4	5	A	A/ Row Average
1	0.54108	1.36119	0.53442	0.52208	0.32175	3.28053	6.06289
2	0.10822	0.27224	0.38173	0.52208	0.25025	1.53452	5.63667
3	0.07730	0.05445	0.07635	0.07458	0.10725	0.38992	5.10738
4	0.07730	0.03889	0.07635	0.07458	0.10725	0.37437	5.01946
5	0.06012	0.03889	0.02545	0.02486	0.03575	0.18507	5.17678
						Average	**5.40064**
						Critical Index	**0.10016**
						Critical Ratio	**0.08943**

Table 4.3: Consistency Matrix Operation

Step 5:

The consistency index (CI) is then computed as the sum obtained from step 4 subtract the number of items being compared (n) and divided by (n −1). So, we obtain a ratio of (5.400637 − 5)/4 = 0.100159.

Step 6:

The consistency ratio (CR) is then obtained as CI/RI where RI is known as random index which is the consistency index of a randomly generated pairwise comparison matrix. For this problem, CR = 0.100159/1.12 = 0.0894. Since this value is 0.10 or less, it is considered acceptable. We can therefore, conclude that the QFD team is consistent in its judgement. Otherwise, we need to identify the source of the inconsistency and follow the iterative procedures provided by Madu [1994] to resolve this conflict before arriving at an acceptable priority indexes for customer requirement items. The random index is given in Table 4.4 below as follows:

N	3	4	5	6	7	8
RI	0.58	0.90	1.12	1.24	1.32	1.41

Table 4.4: Random Index Table

Now that we have validated the consistency of QFD team in obtaining the priority indexes, we can apply them in the QFD. We shall go back to Figure 3-4 and replace the 'importance to customer'

weights used in that problem with the 'customer priority indexes' we
have just generated. Thus, we obtain Figure 4-2 as shown below:

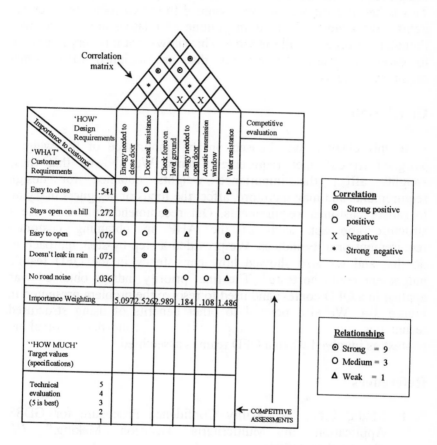

Figure 4.2: QFD and AHP

Based on these new priority indices, we see that the most important
design requirement should be 'energy needed to close door' followed
by 'check force on level ground' and 'door seal resistance.' The least
important is 'acoustic transmission window.' We should however,
point out that this example is for illustrative purposes only. The intent
of using the AHP in this chapter is to show that it is a more structure
approach and will increase the likelihood of making the correct weight

assignments to customer requirement items. As seen from this example, as the weights change so will the focus on design requirements. In Figure 3-4 for example, we observe that the order of design requirements is different from the order observed in Figure 4-2. This is because the weights we assigned to the customer requirement items have changed in their magnitude of relative importance even though their order is still the same. This shows that it is very important to carefully assess the weights that are assigned to customer requirement items.

Conclusion

In this chapter, we focused on the importance of the weights assigned to customer requirement items. We showed that these weights affect the importance weights obtained for design requirements and may therefore, affect the focus of designers in trying to satisfy customer requirements. Our recommendation is to use a structure approach such as the AHP in obtaining customer requirement priority indices. We provided a step-by-step approach to do that and we also showed how consistency in the QFD team's judgement could be tested. The final priority indices obtained was applied in a QFD context and used to resolve the problem presented in Figure 3-4. We also pointed to other benefits of using structured techniques such as the AHP especially in a group decision-making context as involved when a QFD team is assembled.

References

1. Madu, C.N., "A Quality Confidence Procedure for GDSS Application in Multicriteria Decision Making," *IIE Transactions* (1994).
2. Saaty, T.L., "Rank Generation, Preservation, and Reversal in the Analytic Hierarchy Decision Process," *Decision Sciences* 18 (1987), 157-177.

Chapter 5

5.0   QFD AND BENCHMARKING

In Figure 3-4, we provided a competitive assessment of company X against companies A and B. This assessment is helpful in evaluating company X performance against its competitors. This chapter focuses on the integration of benchmarking in QFD. This linkage will help the QFD team to design and produce superior products and services for its customers. First, we explore the meaning and definitions of benchmarking. Chen and Paetsch [1998] provide an excellent introduction to benchmarking. The origins of benchmarking in business practices can be traced to Xerox Corporation. Xerox used benchmarking as one of its quality techniques to successfully overcome the Japanese competitive challenges in the late 1970s and the middle 1980s. Since then, several other major corporations around the world have gracefully adopted different forms of benchmarking. Notable among these companies are Ford Corporation, AT & T, Texas Instrument, and Lexus. As benchmarking techniques have grown popular so have the definitions of benchmarking. One of the earliest definitions of benchmarking is from Xerox. As expected, benchmarking has its origins from the corporate world and most of the definitions have also come from the corporate world rather than academia. Some of the definitions are presented below:

Xerox: "continuous process of measuring our products, services and practices against our toughest competition or those companies recognised as world leaders."

Ford Corporation: "a structured approach for learning from others and applying that knowledge."

Texas Instruments: "a quality improvement tool that enables us to measure our products, services and practices against those of our toughest competitors or other leading companies."

AT & T: "continuous process of measuring our current business operations and comparing them to best in-class companies."

3M: "tool used to search for enablers that allow a company to perform at best-in-class level in a business process."

What is clear from this is that there is no universal definition of benchmarking for business practices. Each corporation defines it as it suits their needs and goals. However, one common theme in all these definitions is the focus on learning from the best in class to improve performance. There are several other definitions of benchmarking, which reiterate most of the definitions given by business. These definitions have generally come from researchers [Grayson (1994), Madu and Kuei (1995), and Spendolini (1992).

5.1 Types of Benchmarking

There are four major types of benchmarking that was originally offered by Xerox. These are namely, internal, competitive, functional and generic. Internal benchmarking involves comparing similar operations within the organization. The focus is inward as a result it may not be possible to achieve the best in class since the sampling frame is limited. As Chen and Paetsh [1998], noted, the potential for improvement through internal benchmarking is modest at 10%. Competitive benchmarking on the other hand involves comparing one against its direct competitors. This is more difficult to achieve because of legal and competitive constraints. The potential for improvement is estimated at about 20%. Functional benchmarking requires comparing ones operation to similar operations in one's own industry. Functional benchmarking is considered to be easy and potential for improvement is in the 30% range. Generic benchmarking involves comparing one's function or activity to any best-in-class performer irrespective of the industry. For example, an auto manufacturer may benchmark LL Bean for its packaging even though they are in different industries. This type of benchmarking is considered easy to implement, the sampling frame is large, and potential for improvement is in the 30% range.

The classification of benchmarking provided above is often referred to as the Xerox model. The focus is more on whom to benchmark. Madu and Kuei [1995] offered an alternative classification scheme. Their scheme, which consists of five types of benchmarking, focus on what is to be benchmarked. This adds to the original classification by Miller et al. (1992). The five categories that emerge are product, functional, best practices, strategic and systemic. Chen and Paetsh [1998] recommended that the best practices could be better-renamed

best management practices. The definitions are adapted from Madu
and Kuei (1995).

5.1.1 Product benchmarking

The focus is to learn from competitive products that are the
best-in-class performers. For example, when Toyota introduced its
luxury Lexus cars, it had to benchmark top performers such as
Mercedes Benz and BMW. The learning gained from this process was
instrumental in designing and producing competitive cars in the
luxury car market.

5.1.2 Functional benchmarking

The focus here is on benchmarking the process rather than the
product. For example, a manufacturer may be interested in learning
specific production processes from recognised leaders. Such processes
may include Just-in-Time, Flexible Manufacturing Systems, or Lean
Production.

5.1.3 Best-Practices Benchmarking

Emphasis here is on management practices. Attention is given
to work related matters such as the role of the work environment on
performance, salary incentives, safety guidelines, etc. General Electric
(GE) is known as a major advocate of best-practices benchmarking.

5.1.4 Strategic benchmarking

The emphasis here is on the overall business strategy of the
organisation. It is checked for consistency and compared to results
derived from other benchmarking practices.

5.1.5 Systemic benchmarking

This goes beyond the normal business strategy to include
overall organisational performance. The organisation caters to the
global needs of its customers by laying emphasis on environmental
protection and social responsibility issues. The goal is to learn from
the practices of organisations that are leaders in environmental
protection and social responsibility issues.

An organisation can improve its performance through the process
of benchmarking. The traditional application of QFD has been in the

area of product or service design. However, QFD application is being extended to a variety of organisational activities. Companies can use QFD for both their internal and external activities to identify critical activities to focus on to improve their performance. Each of the five types of benchmarking discussed above can form an object of QFD assessment by a QFD cross-functional team. For example, with systemic benchmarking, a company may try to understand external needs of both internal and external customers as they relate to the natural environment and match those needs with design requirements. In fact, the company will be more competitive if it takes a holistic posture of its products and activities rather than focusing on the direct product alone. Thus, QFD can be applied not only in designing product quality but also in integrating environmental factors in the product design, improving the efficiency of production activity, and in achieving corporate social responsibility. In the next section, we will discuss the benchmarking component of the "House of Quality" namely the competitive and the engineering evaluations.

5.2   Competitive Evaluation

From Figure 3-4, we construct Figure 5-1, which is the competitive assessment matrix. This matrix allows QFD team to position their products or services against that of the company's major competitors.

The type of benchmarking employed here is product benchmarking. Company X is comparing its product against those of companies A and B identified as its major competitors. We can take each of the customer requirement items one at a time and see how well company X is doing when compared to its major competitors. First, with "easy to close," we notice that company X is doing very poorly when compared to companies A and B. Although companies A and B are doing much better, they still need to improve on this item since none of them appears to be getting the top score of 5. Furthermore, from Figures 3-4 and 4-2, we observe that 'easy to close' is the most important customer requirement. This should be a major concern to company X since it can not be competitive if it fails to satisfy this important customer requirement. Obviously, company X needs to benchmark company B and then, try to surpass it on this customer requirement item by targeting to achieve a score of 5.

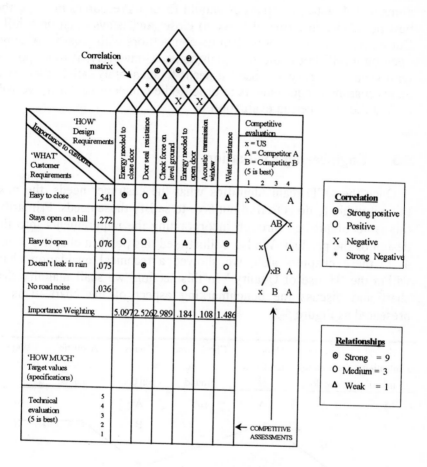

Figure 5.1: QFD and Benchmarking

Next to 'easy to close' in the order of importance to the customer is 'stays open on a hill.' Company X appears to be doing very well and much better than companies A and B. Companies A and B have comparable performance. However, company X still needs improvement to achieve the score of 5. From Table 5-1, it is apparent also that company X trails its competitors in the remaining customer requirement items although they are of less significance as shown in Table 4-2.

Based on the information derived from this benchmarking analysis and the relative priorities assigned to customer requirement items in Table 4-2, company X should focus its resources in being the best performer in terms of 'easy to close' and 'stays open on a hill.' Currently, it is doing better than its competitors with regards to 'stays open on a hill' but could do much better. Conversely, it trails poorly with regards to 'easy to close.' It needs to adequately satisfy these two major customer requirements in order to be competitive. Next, we will look at the engineering evaluation.

5.3   Engineering Evaluation

Once the QFD team identifies what the customer needs, the next thing it ought to do is to find out how to satisfy those needs. Primarily, this is accomplished through incorporating the requirements into the design of the product. We have illustrated this point in chapters 3 and 4. In these chapters also, we showed a technical evaluation chart within the 'House of Quality.' In this section, we shall magnify that chart and discuss the benchmarking aspect of the chart. This is presented as Figure 5-2.

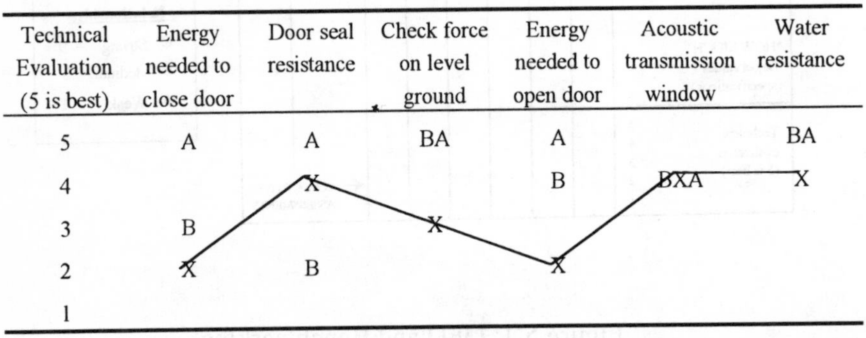

Technical Evaluation (5 is best)	Energy needed to close door	Door seal resistance	Check force on level ground	Energy needed to open door	Acoustic transmission window	Water resistance
5	A	A	BA	A		BA
4		X		B	BXA	X
3	B		X			
2	X	B		X		
1						

Figure 5.2: Technical Evaluation Chart

Notice from Figure 5-2, that there exist a significant technical gap between company X and its competitors companies A and B in almost all the design requirements. For example, company X has a rating score of 2 with respect to the 'energy needed to close door' while company A has a score of 5. Also, notice that from the importance weighting attached to the design requirements, the 'energy needed to close door' is apparently, the most important design requirement needed to achieve customer satisfaction. This technical gap suggests an area that the QFD team must focus on developing sufficient capabilities in order to deliver competitive products or services that will meet customer needs. From Figure 3-4 and 4-2, we observe that the other three major design requirements are 'door seal resistance,' 'check force on level ground,' and 'water resistance.' Company X appears to have sufficient technical capacity to satisfy the design requirements for 'door seal resistance' and 'water resistance' but it is not the industry leader. Company A is the industry leader for both design requirements and shares this leadership role with company B in terms of 'water resistance.' Company X also lacks the technical capacity to 'check force on level ground.' Although it is equally comparable with companies B and A with respect to 'acoustic transmission window,' however, this is the least important design requirement. The engineering benchmarking chart presented in Figure 5-2 clearly shows that company X does not have the technical superiority needed to satisfy the customer requirements. It is transparent from this that the technological gap that exists between company X and its competitors must be significantly narrowed if it intends to satisfy customer needs for the product or service. If this technical gap persists, company X will not be competitive and will not survive in this business. There is an apparent need for quick learning and possibly, re-engineering for company X to survive in this business.

Benchmarking as orchestrated here through QFD is important because it makes the QFD team take a critical role in its company's operations. They come to understand the needs of the customer and the company's lack of competitiveness. Through QFD for example, company X is able to match its strengths and weaknesses against that if its competitors. A detailed study of these strengths and weaknesses could suggest areas for continuous improvement (i.e., those areas with sufficient technical capabilities or high competitive evaluations) and areas for re-engineering (i.e., those areas with significant technical gaps). An appropriate decision may therefore, be needed to either acquire the needed technical capacity in terms of human resources or process changes or to in fact, drop the product line if there is no feasibility for achieving the type of improvement needed to achieve customer satisfaction.

5.4   CONCLUSION

In this chapter, we discussed briefly the origins of benchmarking and the different types of benchmarking. We also illustrated with an example how benchmarking is useful in making competitive and engineering or technical evaluations in a QFD framework. Benchmarking through QFD could help the organisation to identify potential weaknesses and strengths and focus its resources to close technical and competitive gaps when possible. The benchmarking information could also be useful in a decision making environment where there may be need for either continuous improvement or re-engineering. For example, when the company has sufficient technical capacity, it does not relax. Rather, it could gradually continue to improve on its technology until there may be need for a complete overhaul. However, when there is a large technical gap, a quantum leap change or re-engineering will be needed if the company intends to satisfy the customer and become competitive. Without such a rapid reaction to achieve change, the company may never catch up with its competitors let alone surpass them. This may lead to the further demise of the company or a complete withdrawal from that market. Thus, benchmarking through QFD can lead to important decision making. However, the user has to be able to read the information that is being generated through this process. The benchmarking procedure discussed here can be applied at each stage of the QFD development and to any type of benchmarking discussed above.

REFERENCES

1. Chen, I.J., and Paetsch, K.A., "Benchmarking: a quest for continuous improvement," in Handbook of Total Quality Management (ed., Madu, C.N.), Boston, MA: Kluwer Academic Publishers, 1998.
2. Grayson, J., "Back to the basics of benchmarking," *Quality*, May 1994, pp. 20-23.
3. Madu, C.N., and Kuei, C-H., Strategic Total Quality Management, Westport, CT: Quorum Books, 1995.
4. Miller, J.G., et al. Benchmarking Global Manufacturing, Homewood, Ill.: Irwin, 1992.
5. Spendolini, M.J., The Benchmarking Book, NY, NY: AMACOM Press, 1992.

Chapter 6

6.0 QFD AND STRATEGIC PLANNING

In this chapter, we discuss the fit between QFD and strategic planning. Our aim is to show that QFD is closely associated to the overall goal and survivability of the firm. QFD is the driving force behind a firm's business strategy. In the absence of a business strategy, the firm has no purpose, no focus, and can not be in business. Yet, business strategy can not be developed without an understanding of customer needs and the firm's ability to satisfy those needs. The mere existence of a business is often related to its strategy and it is through QFD that business strategies can be made functional. This chapter will expand on this discussion and present a strategic planning framework as a guide.

Every successful business must have a strategic plan. Planning is essential in the management of any organization. As Fayol [1984] noted, planning is a means of "assessing the future and making provision for it." Radford [1980] defined planning as involving three phases: visualizing possible future situations the organization may be involved in; ordering the situations' preferences relative to the objectives of the organization; and contemplating how the most preferred future situation can be accomplished while the least preferred is avoided. There are key points that can be identified from these definitions of planning, namely the need to anticipate the future that the organization may be involved in and developing strategies to deal with that future. Also, the preferences to address the future situations must be ordered and suitable to the objectives of the organization. Clearly, any meaningful organization must have a purpose or a definition for its existence. The organization must offer a product and/or service that will chart its course to the future. Without a purposeful objective, the organization is nonexistent. Once there is a purpose, there must also be demand for that purpose as may be

43

articulated in terms of the product or service that is being offered. For example, companies that offer products or services anticipate to satisfy the demands generated by customers. Governments anticipate public service. Thus, any form of organization must have a purpose, which needs to be broken down in terms of product or service offerings. Furthermore, there must be an audience for whatever service or product that is being offered. However, just having a purpose or the target audience is not enough to sustain this purposeful organization. The organization must make sure that its product or services meet a level of excellence that will guarantee customer satisfaction. Otherwise, the organization risks failure. QFD can therefore, be used as a strategic tool to help an organization chart its course. We shall now discuss the QFD from a strategic perspective. First, we present Figure 6-1, which shows three major steps to incorporating QFD into an organization's strategic plan. These three steps are Preplanning (Business Strategy), Evaluation and Action-Implementation.

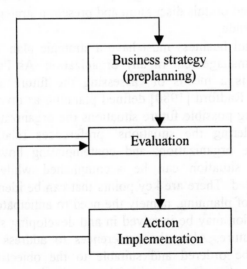

Figure 6-1: Business Strategy Paradigm

As shown in this figure, there is a sequence and this sequence goes in the order presented in Figure 6-1. We first start with a business strategy, then evaluation and then action-implementation. The loops that are shown in this Figure imply that this is an open system that receives feedback through each stage of the process. The feedback received may redirect the QFD team to any of the precedent steps. We shall discuss each step in detail below.

6.1 QFD Paradigm

In this section, we present a strategic framework denoted as the QFD paradigm. The QFD paradigm is a way of thinking through the business strategy of the firm by breaking down the mission to that of satisfying customer needs and showing how this could be done through the methods of quality function deployment.

6.2 Business strategy paradigm (Preplanning)

The business strategy paradigm starts by identifying the broad mission, vision, goals and objectives of the organization. This paradigm will address how management views the organization and outline the organization's boundaries. It is through this doctrine that the mission of the organization can be understood by its members and effectively achieved. Business strategy paradigms must be based on a vision of the firm. The organization must have an understanding of its present position in the industry and where it wants to be in the future and how it intends to get there. Visionary leaders can develop an effective business strategy paradigm that can guide the organization to a promising future. Once the business strategy is developed, it must be frequently evaluated to align it with the dynamic changes in the environment. Companies like Harley-Davidson, Inc., Xerox, and US automobile manufacturers all underwent paradigm shifts in the 1970s and 80s to realign their business strategies to focus on product quality. This shift helped them to regain lost market shares and compete effectively with Japanese companies. One key factor in any business strategy is that it always contains an element of trying to satisfy the customer or winning the confidence of the customer. This can not be done without a breaking down of a business strategy into tactical or operational terms that can be achieved by all units within the organization. The QFD serves that role as its team is made-up of members of the cross-functional units of the organization. The inter-functional nature of the QFD team makes it possible to identify and understand the different world views of the different departments, resolve emerging conflicts that may hinder the ability to achieve organizational goals, and optimize the resources of the organization to achieve a common goal. Through this, redundant activities could be eliminated, optimization rather than sub-optimization will be achieved, and the business of satisfying the customer becomes the business of all functional units within the organization and not just that of the marketing or sales people. Designers are therefore, not afar from the end users. Designers no longer have to offer the customer the product as they see it. Rather, they offer the customer the product as the customer sees it.

Once the missions of the organization are laid out, and the business it is in is spelled out, it is important to identify the product or service features that must be present to satisfy the customer. This is the process of listening to the voice of the customer as we laid out in Chapter 2. Through this process, a list of customer requirements can be identified. We have discussed that it is more important to focus on the significant requirements of the customer rather than on a broad list that may add little or no value to the product or service.

The QFD team must now identify the design requirements to satisfy customer needs. This is more like forming a solution strategy. The list of customer requirements ('whats') offers the problems that the organization must confront to be competitive. However, the design requirements ('hows') show how these problems can be solved. Without knowing the solution techniques, it may not be possible to satisfy customer requirements. Again, this list should focus on relevance. The most significant design requirements should be focused on. As shown, when design requirements are laid out, some correlation may be observed and there may be need for a trade-off.

With both the customer and design requirements identified, it is important to assign target requirements for the design requirements. These target requirements are often specific, measurable and attainable. Priorities should also be established on the customer requirement items to guide the team in ensuring that those critical customer requirements are satisfied.

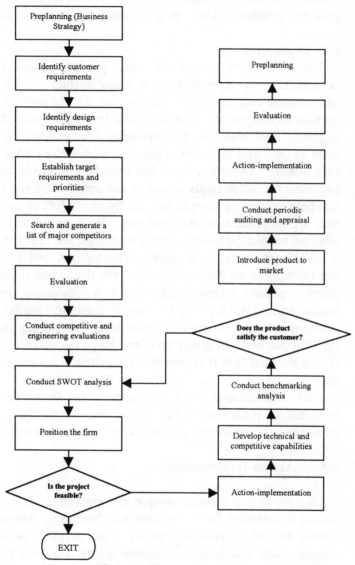

Fig 6-2: QFD Paradigm

These steps are outlined in Figure 6-2. As shown, the next step would be to make a list of major competitors in that product or service line. Again, the aim should be to focus on the key competitors that control a substantial share of the market. It serves no purpose to list all potential competitors who may not have any impact on the market.

6.3 Evaluation

The evaluation phase of this process involves conducting competitive and engineering or technical evaluations. This is a process of benchmarking. Here, the organization tries to position itself against its major competitors. This will help the organization fulfill a major organizational mission. For example, where does the organization want to be? And does the organization have the resources needed to take it there? These questions can only be effectively answered if the organization understands where its competitors are and knows how to compete against its competitors for those product or service attributes that are important to the customer. With an understanding of its position in relation to its major competitors, the firm can now conduct a SWOT (strength, weaknesses, opportunities, and threats) analysis. For example, does the organization have the technical capacity? Can it develop needed technical capacity in a reasonable time? Does the organization fare well in the major customer attributes or design requirements against its competitors? By answering such questions, the firm can better position itself and judge the viability of the project. If it is deemed that it is unrealistic to attain a competitive posture in that product or service line, it may be time to exit. Otherwise, the needed technical and competitive capabilities should be developed. A new design plan should be offered that is internally checked for consistency given design parameters and customer requirements.

6.3   Action-Implementation

This phase will involve sample test marketing. The aim here is to collect information for the purpose benchmarking. Adequate statistical sample should be collected to see if the product satisfies customer requirements, and how it competes against competitors' products or services. When the QFD team is satisfied that this product or service can be competitive, it could then be introduced in a large scale to the market. The introduction of the product is not the end of the process. The product needs to be periodically reviewed and compared against other competitive products, gradual changes in product design may be necessitated overtime to add more value to the product, and information should be continuously collected from the customer to improve product or service quality. "What if analysis" should be frequently conducted to understand the perceptions of the customer when certain product features are either added, enhanced or removed. Knowledge of the market will help determine the right time to replace the product with a newer and more improved product. Information that will be obtained on a timely basis will help the firm continue to produce the product that will meet customer expectations. Notice that Figure 6-2 has a cyclic loop to denote again that this system is open and can be modified with new information.

6.4 QFD Relevance Tree Diagram

We can summarize the content of Figure 6-2 in to a QFD Relevance Tree Diagram shown as Figure 6-3.

Figure 6-3: QFD Relevance tree diagram

This figure shows that the mission and purpose of the organization is to achieve customer satisfaction. This mission is worthwhile since the survival of the organization is directly related to its ability to satisfy and retain its customers. However, this mission can be achieved if certain objectives are satisfied. These objectives include providing products and services that satisfy customer requirements, making efficient use of resources, developing shorter product cycle times, improving product design and quality, etc. While these objectives may lead to achieving the mission, they may not all be easily attainable. Certain constraints may limit the ability to achieve these objectives. Such constraints may include time – if the product can not be introduced timely to regain competitiveness; cost – the cost of introducing a competitive product may be too high; engineering and technical – lack of appropriate technology or skill may make it difficult to effectively satisfy customer requirements; human resources – properly trained human resources may not be available; support – some support services needed may not exist. These constraints must be evaluated on how they can potentially influence the organization's mission and goals and appropriate steps taken to resolve potential conflicts. It is also important to set standards. These standards will be the standards that the product or service must meet in order to be competitive. Such standards should be cognizant of industry standards as well as competitors' standards. Thus, competitive and engineering benchmarking should be undertaken in order to set these standards.

6.5 PLAN-DO-CHECK-ACT (PDCA) cycle

The discussions outlined in this chapter are similar to the PDCA cycle made popular by Deming. This is shown in Figure 6-4. Madu and Kuei [1995] refer to it as the strategic cycle. Clearly, it is obvious from this discussion and Figure 6-2 in particular, that the PLAN – is initiated by identifying the business strategy of the firm. This plan articulates the mission and purpose of the firm and how it intends to achieve it. A clear purpose of a business organization will be to satisfy customer requirements through the delivery of acceptable product or service. The method to achieve this mission will be to design customer requirements into the product or service. We have shown that the QFD can help us to achieve that goal. The DO involves the actual design of the product. The product is designed taken into consideration customer requirements, technical feasibility, and target values or standards that may have been established. The CHECK involves a comparative analysis of the product and the design requirements with that of competitors. Benchmarking is conducted at this stage to ensure that the product competes effectively with existing products in the market. Also, test marketing is conducted after the product is produced. This involves statistical sampling surveys to compare the newly designed product or the new product with major competitor's product. Market testing of the product is limited to a statistical sample drawn from the population of potential customers for the product. Information gained through this process can be used to improve the product before its large-scale introduction to the market. The ACT deals with the large-scale introduction to the market. This does not mark the end of the process. Information gathering is important through the life of the product. New competitive information should always be obtained and the product should be continuously benchmarked against leading brands. Furthermore, the QFD team should continue to listen to the voice of the customer to know when new features should be added to the product or a replacement product may be offered. In addition, the 'unspoken' attributes that may add value to the product should be continuously investigated as the QFD team seeks to constantly improve the quality of the product. This is a never-ending process with the overall goal of continuously improving the quality of the product or service so that customer satisfaction can be achieved.

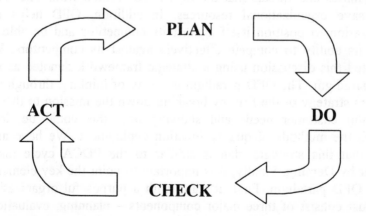

PLAN

ACT

DO

CHECK

Figure 6-4: Plan-Do-Check-Act (PDCA) cycle

In the end, the organization is better able to deal with customer reality. The survivability of the firm rests on its ability to satisfy customer requirements. By maintaining a process that frequently monitors the product, continuously improves it by adding features that add value to the customer, the product will be able to satisfy the needs of the customer. When the product satisfies the needs of the customer, the firm becomes competitive and can gain market shares through customer loyalty. The firm will stay in business and will be able to survive and continue to offer valuable services to its customers. The QFD is indeed an important quality tool that can help guide the firm to achieve its mission.

6.6 Conclusion

In this chapter, we showed that the QFD is an important quality tool in achieving the strategic goals of the firm. Clearly, the purpose of business organizations is to provide quality products and services to its customers. It is only through the attainment of that goal that these businesses can survive. The QFD approach takes a strategic perspective of the business by helping the firm to understand the needs of the customer and how those needs could be satisfied. It also helps the firm to position itself against its competitors so that proper decisions could be made on the direction of the firm. These decisions are based on thorough analysis of the strengths, weaknesses, opportunities and threats that the firm is confronted with. The QFD helps save organizational resources. In addition, QFD helps the organization to position itself against its competitor and be able to assess its ability to compete effectively against its competitors. We presented this discussion using a strategic framework denoted as the QFD paradigm. The QFD paradigm is a way of thinking through the business strategy of the firm by breaking down the mission to that of satisfying customer needs and showing how this could be done through the methods of quality function deployment. We have also noted that this strategic plan is similar to the PDCA cycle made popular by Deming. Finally, it is important to point the key elements of the QFD paradigm. First, it starts with a purposeful organization and must consist of three major components – planning, evaluation, and action-implementation. Second, the three phases of the QFD paradigm are inter-dependent. Third, the ability to collect timely feedback is essential to the successful use of the QFD paradigm. The use of feedback information is necessary to achieve continuous improvement in the product design and production. This paradigm operates as an open system and is able to receive information from its operating environment to help improve the quality of decisions that are made. Finally, the goal is to achieve customer satisfaction.

References

1. Fayol, H., <u>General and Industrial Management</u>, NY, NY: Institute of Electrical and Electronics Engineers, 1984.
2. Madu, C.N., and Kuei, C-H., <u>Strategic Total Quality Management</u>, Westport, CT: Quorum Books, 1995.
3. Radford, K.J., <u>Strategic Planning: An Analytical Approach</u>, Reston, VA: Reston Publishing Co., 1980.

Chapter 7

7.0 QFD AND STATISTICAL QUALITY CONTROL

The ultimate goal of QFD is to produce goods and services that will meet customer requirement needs. In chapter 6, we showed that QFD fits into the firm's strategic planning. Strategic planning deals with a broad range of issues that can be better summarized by the plan-do-check-act. In this chapter, we shall start by dissecting some sections of the planning to their operational forms with questions like: how does the firm ensure that the product or service produced is meeting the pre-specified targets? For example, in Figure 3-4, one of the target values especially with respect to the major design requirement "Energy needed to close door" was "Reduce energy level to 7.5 ft/lb." This target must be measurable and otherwise, we can not be sure that this target value is being achieved. We also, will not be able to benchmark it against our competitors since the benchmarking phase will become entirely subjective. In this chapter, we discuss statistical quality control and how it is integrated in a QFD framework.

As we have seen so far, QFD provides a design strategy for the product or service. It does not really provide the actual production of the product or service. However, the design is like the foundation of any production process. If the design is faulty, then the production process will not have a strong foundation to support it. A house without a strong foundation will eventually collapse. Ensuring that the customer's requirements are met is a multi-faceted process in which designing customer requirements into the product or service as provided by QFD is one aspect. For example, in a production system, the design may be sound and articulate all customer requirements however, if the incoming raw material is poor or the production process itself is incapable of meeting specifications, then customer requirements will not be satisfied. QFD as a tool works well when it is integrated with other tools that will lead to the production and delivery

55

of quality products and services to the customer. Statistical quality control is one tool that is traditionally used for this purpose and in this chapter, we shall discuss the application. Statistical quality control comprises of two parts: acceptance sampling and statistical process control.

7.1 Acceptance sampling

Acceptance sampling is normally used to test the quality of incoming raw materials or the quality of outgoing products. For example, a vendor may set a specification with the manufacturer that the "energy needed to close door" should be between 7.5 ± 0.025 ft/lb. Furthermore, in a lot of 1000 shipments, a random sample of 100 items will be tested. If 3 or more are found to be outside the specified range for the "energy needed to close the door", the entire lot will be rejected. Otherwise, it will be accepted. Notice here, that an acceptable standard has been established. This is based on the information derived from QFD that showed that this energy level would be acceptable to the customer. To ensure, that this target is met, the vendor inspects incoming lot by taking samples. These samples are usually random sample since they must represent the entire lot. If from the sample, it is detected that 3 or more items do not meet the standard, the entire lot (not just the sample) is rejected. This is known as acceptance sampling because, it is either that the lot is accepted or rejected. The decision to either reject or accept a lot is known as *lot sentencing*. Notice that here, we did not inspect the entire lot. Yet, we are able to pass judgment on the quality of the lot. The use of random sampling as we have done here has some merit. First, if the sample taken is a random sample or simple random sample, it will be a typical representation of the lot. By simple random sample, each item in the lot will have equal chance of being included in the sample. Also, the use of random sample rather than 100% inspection of the lot is very efficient. It is economical, saves time, and it is less prone to errors. Contrary to our intuition, 100 % inspection does not really guarantee that more accurate decisions will be made. One major problem is that for a large population of products, it becomes almost impossible to achieve 100 % inspection. Human error due to fatigue and equipment malfunction may all make it possible not to obtain reliable inspection results. In addition, there are certain products that can not be subjected to 100 % inspection. A few examples include bombs, light bulbs, and all items that may be destroyed during inspection. There are many ways to design acceptance sampling. We shall refer the reader to [Madu 1998]. We shall focus in this chapter on statistical process control since its use is common in assembly line operations. Clearly, assembly line operations may exist in either a manufacturing or service outlet. For example, banks and cafeterias to name a few use assembly line formats.

7.2 Statistical Process Control

Statistical process control (SPC) is primarily based on the use of graphical displays known as control charts to detect shift in the process from design specifications. This is used widely for work in progress or work in process. When a shift is observed from the design specification, corrective actions are taken immediately. It could be seen that this is different from acceptance sampling since in that case, inspection is done on the finished or incoming product and not while the production process is on. The use of SPC can help to reduce waste, and maximize the use of valuable resources. The objective of SPC is to improve the entire production process by ensuring that the process is on target in meeting customer requirements as identified through design requirements in QFD phase. SPC is based on the assumption that natural variation is inherent in any process. The occurrence of natural variation is expected and should not be cause for alarm. For example, the target to "reduce energy level to 7.5 ft/lb." has to leave room for the occurrence of natural variation. Without consideration of such variation, it may be almost impossible to achieve that target. Thus, we could specify an acceptable range within this target value by stating this specification goal as 7.5 ± 0.025 ft/lb.

Dr. Walter Shewhart introduced SPC at Bell Laboratories in the 1920s. He identified two causes of variations: common or natural causes of variation and special or assignable causes of variation. Common or natural causes of variation can be explained by chance occurrence and may not be easily controlled. For example, temperature, pressure or humidity may affect the strength of material. Product quality may be influenced by the source of the raw material. Poor process design and a poor work environment may affect the production of quality products. Some aspects of the common causes of variation may be due to the state of nature and may be inherently uncontrollable. However, there are some aspects that can be controlled. For example, the influence of poor work environment on the production of quality goods and services can be controlled. Likewise, the influence of poor incoming raw material on the quality of the finished product can be controlled. However, the authority to exert control on common causes of variation rests with top management. The production worker on the assembly floor has no control over these issues and lacks the authority to effect a change. The tools he or she is provided to do the work limit the production worker and the lack of the right tool can affect the ability to produce quality product or service. The aim of this is to quit blaming the production worker for all the problems with the product. A more holistic orientation should be resorted in order to identify the source of the problem. Obviously, management can effect a change by changing suppliers or replacing poorly designed processes.

Conversely, the operator is responsible for the special or assignable causes of variation. Such variation may occur because the operator is not properly trained and therefore, does not have the necessary skill to do the job, operator error along the production line, etc. Operators can do something to remove the occurrence of assignable causes of variation. They may need to get better training, or develop the skills needed to operate effectively. Statistical process control identifies only assignable causes of variation so those operators can take corrective actions. When the only variation observed is natural, then, the process is said to be stable and operating under statistical control. The process is predictable when it is stable. It will then satisfy customer requirements and meet customer expectations. Statistical control charts as presented below, are therefore, used to detect when a process is out of control.

7.2   Types of Measurement

Before we discuss the control charts, we shall mention that there are two types of measurements in quality control: measurement by attributes and measurement by variables. *Measurement by attributes* is applicable when the product or service characteristic of interest is discrete or can be categorically stated. For example, suppose we go back to the specifications in Figure 3-4 and we take the specification for "Door seal resistance." Our focus may be to check if the specification is being maintained. Here, the specification is to "Maintain current level." When a sample is inspected, we may simply check 'yes' if the current level is maintained and 'no' if it is not maintained. Other classifications include 'accept' or 'reject,' 0 or 1, win or lose, etc. When the quality characteristic of a product or service can be accessed in a categorical form as this, we have measurement by attributes. *Measurement by variables* on the other hand, deals with a situation where the quality characteristic of the product is expressed in a continuous scale. For example, the energy level needed to open or close the door is given as 7.5 ± 0.025 ft/lb. Normally, when the measurement scale is expressed in a continuous scale such as weight, height, time, temperature, length, etc., it is better to use measurement by variables. Measurement by variables provides more information than measurement by attributes. As a result, measurement by variables will be more powerful than measurement by attributes.

We shall use the example given in Figure 3-4 and provide one example for each measurement types and a general discussion on the use of control charts.

7.3   Control Charts

As we mentioned at the beginning of this chapter, control charts are graphical displays that are used to detect shifts from design specifications. These shifts may be due to special or assignable causes of variation. The aim is to enable operators to take corrective actions while the process is ongoing. Such actions will aim to bring the process back to conformance. Standard control charts will normally have three horizontal lines namely the lower control limit (LCL), the centerline which will be the process mean, and the upper control limit (UCL). Measurements are then taken from the process and plotted on the charts as shown with dots in Figure 7-1. Points that may fall outside the LCL and the UCL may indicate non-conformance with design specification. Conversely, points that fall within the LCL and UCL may indicate conformance with design specifications.

The construction of the control chart is based on statistical principles. It is assumed that the natural variations observed from a process can be explained by the normal probability distribution. As a result, it is important to have a high probability that samples taken from the process will fall within the control limits. The standard practice in establishing control limits is to set it at ± 3 standard deviations of the mean. This will imply that 99.7% of the process output is expected to fall within the control limits while only 0.3% of the process output is expected to fall outside the control limit when the process is stable or in statistical control. We shall now present the examples for each measurement type.

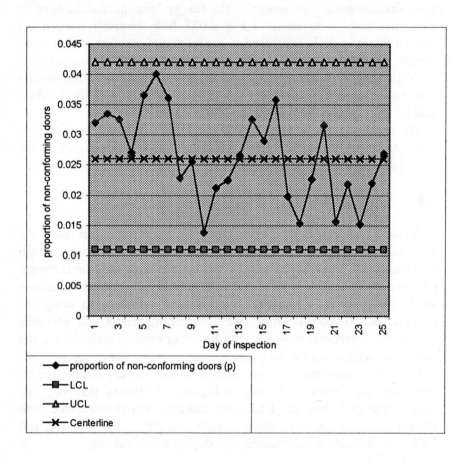

Figure 7.1: X-Bar Chart

7.3.1   Statistical process control charts for attributes

We shall discuss the use of the p-chart as a statistical process control chart for attributes. The p-chart is applicable when it is important to investigate the proportion or fraction of non-conforming items. In our case, we investigated the proportion of non-conforming doors. That is, the proportions of doors that may not maintain the current level for door seal resistance. From Table 1 for example, we observe that on Day 1, 1000 doors were inspected and 32 of them did not maintain the current level for door seal resistance. This gives a proportion of 0.032. Any time we are interested in the fraction or proportion of defective items, the p-chart will be applicable as a control chart. There are other types of control charts for attributes such as the c-chart, np-chart, and the u-chart. These charts are all somewhat related. We shall refer the reader again to Madu [1998]. We shall however, focus on the p-chart. We define the proportion (p) as follows:

$$p \; = \; \frac{\text{Total number of non-conforming doors}}{\text{Total number of doors inspected}} \qquad \cdot \; \cdot \; (7.1)$$

We shall refer to this as the centerline. Using the centerline, which is the average, the control limits can be established as follows:

Lower control limit (LCL) for p

$$LCL(p) = p - 3\left(\sqrt{\frac{p(1-p)}{n}} \right) \qquad \cdots \cdots \cdots \cdots \; (7.2)$$

Upper control limit (UCL) for p

$$UCL(p) = p + 3\left(\sqrt{\frac{p(1-p)}{n}} \right) \qquad \cdots \cdots \cdots \cdots \; (7.3)$$

Note also that if there is a target p value, that target value will replace the p obtained from equation (7.1) as the centerline. We shall illustrate with an example. In the case considered here, the interest is to find the proportion of doors that did not maintain the current level for door seal resistance. From Table 7-1, we observe the record of 25 days of inspection. On the average, the proportion of non-conforming doors is 0.026 over the 25-day period. Using equations (7.2) and (7.3), the LCL and the UCL are obtained as 0.011 and 0.042 respectively for the

Day Number	Number of doors inspected	Number of non-conforming doors	Proportion of non-conforming doors (p)	LCL	UCL	Centerline
1	1000	32	0.032	0.011	0.042	0.026
2	985	33	0.034	0.011	0.042	0.026
3	889	29	0.033	0.011	0.042	0.026
4	925	25	0.027	0.011	0.042	0.026
5	1013	37	0.037	0.011	0.042	0.026
6	998	40	0.040	0.011	0.042	0.026
7	1025	37	0.036	0.011	0.042	0.026
8	875	20	0.023	0.011	0.042	0.026
9	980	25	0.026	0.011	0.042	0.026
10	1010	14	0.014	0.011	0.042	0.026
11	988	21	0.021	0.011	0.042	0.026
12	1022	23	0.023	0.011	0.042	0.026
13	864	23	0.027	0.011	0.042	0.026
14	920	30	0.033	0.011	0.042	0.026
15	965	28	0.029	0.011	0.042	0.026
16	1005	36	0.036	0.011	0.042	0.026
17	855	17	0.020	0.011	0.042	0.026
18	976	15	0.015	0.011	0.042	0.026
19	970	22	0.023	0.011	0.042	0.026
20	1012	32	0.032	0.011	0.042	0.026
21	958	15	0.016	0.011	0.042	0.026
22	1005	22	0.022	0.011	0.042	0.026
23	988	15	0.015	0.011	0.042	0.026
24	1000	22	0.022	0.011	0.042	0.026
25	892	24	0.027	0.011	0.042	0.026
Total	24120	637	0.659			
Averages	964.8	25.48	0.026			

Table 7.1: Proportion of Non-conforming Doors

proportion of non-conforming doors. This computation is shown in Figure 7.1. It is indeed, the p-control chart for this problem. Looking at the chart, it is seen that all the proportion of non-conforming doors fall within the control limits, However, we notice that on Day 6, the proportion of non-conforming doors seem to be very close to the UCL. Naturally, we will prefer a situation where the proportion of non-conforming doors is closer to zero. Notice also, that in computing the LCL, it is possible to obtain a negative value for LCL. When that occurs, we set the LCL to zero. Also, in our computation, we used the average sample size of 964.8 since the number of doors inspected varies from day to day. If the same number is inspected each day, we can simply use that number since its average will also be n. In analyzing the p-chart of Figure 7-1, we observe that all the points fall within the control limits. We may therefore, conclude that the process is stable or operating within statistical control. Therefore, the variations we observed from day to day about the proportion of non-conforming doors are normal and can be explained by chance. When we observe out-of-control points, we try to understand the cause and the source of the variation so that the process can be corrected and brought to conformance.

7.3.2 Statistical process control charts for variables

We will now look at one of the most popular control charts (X-bar and R charts). The X-bar and R charts are based on the sample means and ranges of subgroups of samples to detect process precision and accuracy. The sample mean is used to measure accuracy while to the process's location and the range measures the precision or process variability. The range, rather than the standard deviation, provides timely field information on the variability of the process. The subgroup size is normally kept small say less than five. When the subgroup size is large say (n > 10), it is preferable to use the standard deviation to compute the control limits.

In this section, we take samples of four each time to inspect the energy level to open door. The energy level needed to close door is measured in ft/lb. The target level desired is 7.5 ft/lb. The samples obtained after a 20 day-operation are contained in Table 7-2.

Sample Number	1	2	3	4	Average X	Range (R)	UCL	LCL	Range mean	UCL	LCL	Centerline	X-bar
1	7.49	7.52	7.45	7.56	7.5050	0.11	0.16	0	0.071	7.55	7.45	7.50	7.51
2	7.48	7.59	7.55	7.51	7.5325	0.11	0.16	0	0.071	7.55	7.45	7.50	7.53
3	7.50	7.42	7.48	7.50	7.4750	0.08	0.16	0	0.071	7.55	7.45	7.50	7.48
4	7.53	7.45	7.58	7.49	7.5125	0.13	0.16	0	0.071	7.55	7.45	7.50	7.51
5	7.49	7.51	7.56	7.45	7.5025	0.11	0.16	0	0.071	7.55	7.45	7.50	7.50
6	7.46	7.53	7.55	7.49	7.5075	0.09	0.16	0	0.071	7.55	7.45	7.50	7.51
7	7.45	7.52	7.52	7.56	7.5125	0.11	0.16	0	0.071	7.55	7.45	7.50	7.51
8	7.48	7.55	7.48	7.53	7.5100	0.07	0.16	0	0.071	7.55	7.45	7.50	7.51
9	7.52	7.51	7.55	7.50	7.5200	0.05	0.16	0	0.071	7.55	7.45	7.50	7.52
10	7.44	7.48	7.49	7.47	7.4700	0.05	0.16	0	0.071	7.55	7.45	7.50	7.47
11	7.50	7.51	7.50	7.52	7.5075	0.02	0.16	0	0.071	7.55	7.45	7.50	7.51
12	7.59	7.50	7.49	7.52	7.5250	0.10	0.16	0	0.071	7.55	7.45	7.50	7.53
13	7.52	7.49	7.55	7.49	7.5125	0.06	0.16	0	0.071	7.55	7.45	7.50	7.51
14	7.52	7.51	7.55	7.51	7.5225	0.04	0.16	0	0.071	7.55	7.45	7.50	7.52
15	7.49	7.50	7.50	7.52	7.5025	0.03	0.16	0	0.071	7.55	7.45	7.50	7.50
16	7.55	7.50	7.55	7.56	7.5400	0.06	0.16	0	0.071	7.55	7.45	7.50	7.54
17	7.52	7.52	7.50	7.54	7.5200	0.04	0.16	0	0.071	7.55	7.45	7.50	7.52
18	7.53	7.55	7.50	7.51	7.5225	0.05	0.16	0	0.071	7.55	7.45	7.50	7.52
19	7.53	7.50	7.49	7.50	7.5050	0.04	0.16	0	0.071	7.55	7.45	7.50	7.51
20	7.51	7.49	7.51	7.56	7.5175	0.07	0.16	0	0.071	7.55	7.45	7.50	7.52
Average					7.511125	0.071	0.16						

Table 7.2: Samples of Energy Level Needed to Open Doors(lb/ft)

We need to establish the control limits and develop a control chart for this problem. The control limits are defined as follows first for the X-bar chart:

$$LCL = X - A_2R \quad . \quad . \quad . \quad . \quad . \quad . \quad (7.4)$$
$$UCL = X + A_2R \quad . \quad . \quad . \quad . \quad . \quad . \quad (7.5)$$

And for the R chart, we obtain

$$LCL = D_3R \quad . \quad . \quad . \quad . \quad . \quad . \quad . \quad (7.6)$$
$$UCL = D_4R \quad . \quad . \quad . \quad . \quad . \quad . \quad . \quad (7.7)$$

The terms A_2, D_3, and D_4 are obtained from the Table and are reprinted here as Table 7-3.

Number of observations in a subgroup (n)	A_2	D_3	D_4
2	1.88	0.00	3.27
3	1.02	0.00	2.57
4	0.73	0.00	2.28
5	0.58	0.00	2.11
6	0.48	0.00	2.00
7	0.42	0.08	1.92
8	0.37	0.14	1.86
9	0.34	0.18	1.82
10	0.31	0.22	1.78
11	0.29	0.26	1.74
12	0.27	0.28	1.72
13	0.25	0.31	1.69
14	0.24	0.33	1.67
15	0.22	0.35	1.65
16	0.21	0.36	1.64
17	0.20	0.38	1.62
18	0.19	0.39	1.61
19	0.19	0.40	1.60
20	0.18	0.41	1.59

Source: G.L. Grant Quality Control 6th ed. (New York, McGraw Hill, 1988).

<u>Table 7.3: Factors for determining the three-sigma control limits For X bar and R charts</u>

First, we shall present the steps to develop the X-bar and R charts as provided in Madu [98, p.556].

- Compute the sample means for each subgroup;
- Compute the range of each subgroup;
- Compute the mean of all the subgroups. That mean is the grand mean and it is the centerline for the X chart;
- Compute the mean of all the subgroups range. That overall mean is the centerline for the R chart;
- Compute the control limits for R and plot them with the centerline;
- Plot the subgroup's individual R values on the same chart with the centerline and the control limits;
- If no out-of-control points are present in the R chart, then process precision is stable. Otherwise, identify the reasons for variation and take corrective actions;

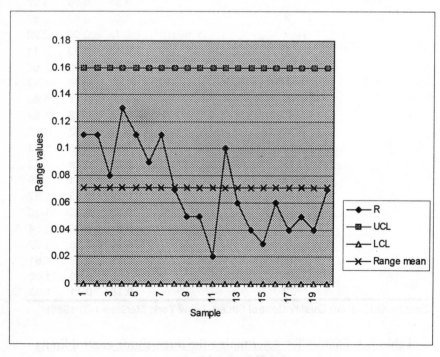

Figure 7.2: R- Chart

- When the process precision is stable, construct the X chart using the centerline and control limits found above;
- Plot the subgroup's respective means on the X chart and check if the process is stable or whether corrective action should be taken. Following these steps, we see from the R-chart given as Figure 7-2, that all the range points for the 20 subgroups fall within the control limits. Therefore, the process precision is stable. Once this is achieved, we proceed to evaluate the process accuracy in targeting an energy level of 7.5 ft/lb.

Figure 7.3 shows that all the points for the 20 subgroups fall within the control limits. Therefore, the process accuracy is stable. Thus, the process is meeting the target of 7.5 ft/lb. for the energy needed to close door. We can now, conclude that the process is stable.

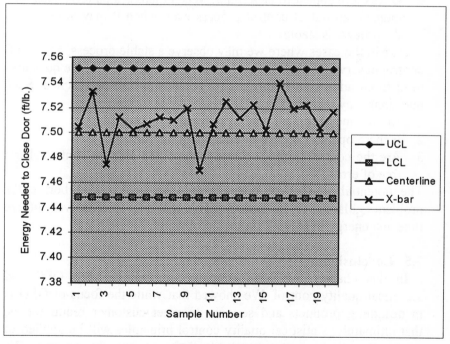

Figure 7.3: X-bar Chart

7.4 Interpretation of control charts

Our discussion of the control charts tend to suggest that once the sample points fall within the control limits, the process will be stable. However, the process will be unstable when the sample points fall outside the control limits. While this is generally true, it is possible for the sample points to fall within the control limits and yet, the process will be unstable. Thus, even an apparently stable process should be carefully evaluated. The following indicators of out-of-control process should be checked as outlined in Madu [1998, p. 561]:

1. Are successive sample points below or above the centerline for six or more samples? This could be explained by problems such as equipment malfunction, work schedule changes, material or operator differences. The sources of variation should be identified and explained to achieve a stable process.
2. Does there appear to be a trend? When there is a pattern, such may indicate an out-of-control process even when it may appear as if the process is stable.

Like in the cases where we may observe a stable process, an out-of-control observance should also be carefully evaluated. Some questions need to be addressed before a firm conclusion can be reached. Such questions may include:

1. Are the measurement readings properly recorded?
2. Is there operator's error or equipment malfunction?
3. Are the control limits accurately computed and the control charts free of errors?

The potential sources of errors should be investigated before the problem is blamed on the process. This will help to effectively utilize time and energy in solving process problems.

7.5 Conclusions

In this chapter, we have developed a link between QFD and statistical quality control. We showed that while the focus of QFD is in designing products and services to meet customer requirements, that ultimately, statistical quality control principles will be applied to ensure that those requirements are designed into the product. We identified acceptance sampling and statistical process control as components of statistical quality control. However, we focused our discussion on statistical process control since it deals with work-in-process or work-in-progress. We again, illustrated with the information derived from our QFD chart (Figure 3-4) how control charts could be applied to the target specifications for the design requirements. The control charts presented focused on the use of measurement by attributes (p – chart) and measurement by variables (R and X-bar charts). We also discussed briefly how to interpret control charts.

References

Madu, C.N., "Statistical quality control," in Handbook of Total Quality Management (ed. Madu, C.N.), Boston, MA: Kluwer Academic Publishers, 1998.

70

Chapter 8

8.0 STAKEHOLDER VS. CUSTOMER IN PRODUCT DESIGN

In the previous chapters, we have focused our attention on identifying customer requirements and having such requirements satisfied through design. That focus tends to suggest a product-dependent analysis of customer requirements. Indeed, such is true. However, QFD's role can be expanded beyond that. Companies listen to the voice of the customer so they can compete and survive in business. QFD is just a tool that could help them achieve the goal of designing customer requirements into the product or service. In this chapter, we shall expand the definition of customer. Here, we define a customer as anyone or entity that is affected by the product or service offered by a firm. To avoid any confusion in the use of terminology, we shall refer to this class of customers as stakeholders. Thus, stakeholders are individuals or groups that are affected by the products or services offered by a firm. This definition of stakeholders will lead us to our new line of thoughts on how QFD's role in product design could further help the firm to be more competitive.

8.1 The Role of Stakeholders in the Market Place

It is important that firms understand who their customers are and what influence their purchase decisions. Obviously, the essence of any business is to satisfy the customer and by so doing, customer loyalty can be maintained. The customer will continue to patronise the business and that business will not only continue to survive but will thrive and do well financially. Successful businesses attract more investors and are able to generate new capital for re-investment. Thus, businesses that have high customer loyalty tend to also grow faster. However, when a business fails to maintain customer loyalty, it will continue to report financial loses, become a riskier investment and shareholders lose confidence and pull out from the business. Thus, the survival of any business can be linked directly to the business's ability to retain customers.

However, since the 1980s, the market environment has gradually changed. In the past, a customer could assess the quality of a product or service by checking for certain attributes that relate directly to the performance of the product. Once such attributes are maintained at a high quality standard, the customer's business is assured. This is no longer so. Customers no longer look only at the intrinsic product quality attributes. In fact, many customers tend to assume that such attributes should be basic requirements for products. They however, look at other factors such as, the environmental content of the product or service (i.e., energy consumption, pollution, recyclability, etc.) and may in fact, look at the overall performance of the business in other areas such as social responsibility to the community [2]. In other words, focusing on designing products or services that meet the intrinsic needs of the customer may not be enough to gain market shares, maintain customer loyalty and survive in today's business environment. Businesses need to adopt a more holistic view of their operations and guided by vision, will be able to identify the core factors that drive customers to support a business. Such core factors should be integrated in product design in order to satisfy the customer. This goal can be achieved if rather than trying to satisfy customer requirements through QFD, the firm aims to satisfy stakeholder requirements. It should be noted that stakeholder requirements also include the intrinsic needs of the customer that must be present in any product or service offered by the firm. However, it goes beyond that to include extraneous factors that may be part of the "unspoken" requirements of the customer. In this era of information age, customers are more enlightened and well educated. They are asking questions and easily getting answers.

The Internet and other mediums for communication have also helped in making information instantly available to customers. They are taking more proactive roles in their lives and are responding by taking actions to protect their interests. One area in which customers have shown increased focus is in the area of environmental protection and to ignore it will be to ignore the future. Furthermore, social responsibility and integrity issues are becoming prominent in assessing the performance of a firm. Madu and Kuei (1995) introduced the concept of strategic total quality management and defined it as a quality measure of the overall performance of the firm. This performance assessment is not limited to the intrinsic values offered by a product or service but also on how the product or service affects the quality of life of people around it. The growing importance of social responsibility and environmental protection issues can also be seen from the increase in growth of social choices stocks. Evidently, business survives if it is able to satisfy customers by meeting customer requirements and customer requirements do not have to be limited to the direct value derived from the product. For example, a customer purchasing a toner cartridge for a laser printer may be interested in the quality of the print (i.e., clarity and brightness), duration of the cartridge (i.e. number of pages printed), etc. He may at the same time, be concerned with the emission of gases or chemical substances from the cartridge, disposal of expired cartridges. We shall elaborate more on this and why and how QFD teams should respond. A recent case in point is the call by privacy groups such as Junkbusters and Electronic Privacy Information Centre to boycott Intel products over new technology by Intel that would identify consumers as they surf through the Internet. These groups argue that customer profiles will be collected and sold through this new technology. This action has attracted publicity as some lawmakers are calling on Intel to reconsider the introduction of this product [1]. The need to advocate stakeholder analysis in product design can also be supported by studies that show consumers are increasingly willing to pay more for environmentally friendly products [4,5]. Also, the proliferation of new environmental laws most of which have come about as a result of public outrage over the degradation of the environment suggest a need for corporate rethinking of environmental policies [3]. Many companies are indeed seeing environmental and corporate social responsibility programs as good for business today. Hence, we hear of companies introducing new environmental products like the plan to introduce electric cars; the use of genetically engineered micro-organisms to absorb carbon dioxide; marketing of industrial equipment that absorb sulphur oxides and nitrous oxides from smoke stacks of steel and electric power plants; increased use of sewage-control and sludge-treatment equipment to avoid ocean dumping of wastes; low-emission incinerators for both liquid and solid wastes to combat the landfill problems [2]. Indeed, corporations are taking notice of these emerging customer requirements and are also doing something about it. Several companies now have in-house programs to deal with environmental issues. For example, 3M maintains an environmental program known as the 3Ps – Pollution Prevention Pays; Chevron maintains a program known as SMART – Save Money And Reduce Toxic, and Dow Chemical maintains a program known as WRAP – Waste Reduction

Always Pays. In addition, the increasing attention given by more than 100 countries to ISO 14000 series of environmental management systems shows that it is about time to consider other factors beyond the direct product quality.

Corporate alliance with interest groups is also on the rise. For example, the fast-food restaurant giant McDonald's had an alliance with the Environmental Defence Fund (EDF) to develop a way to reduce solid waste. The result is a switch from polystyrene shells to paper wrap. Pacific Gas and Electric Company often seeks the advice of Natural Resources Defence Council. New England Electric System worked with The Conservation Law Foundation to develop its twenty-year strategic plan [3]. This resulted in a focus on the use of renewable resources and recycling of wastes to generate electricity. These alliances are healthy for the businesses because they help increase the competitiveness of the firm. The corporation adopts a holistic perspective of its environment and works with those whose actions and reactions may affect the successful introduction of a product. When the QFD team is expanded to include not just members of the cross-functional units in a firm but stakeholders often referred to as active participants, the opposing views of both groups can be better understood by team members. It is possible that some of the concerns of the stakeholder team may not be effectively treated through design. In that case, other remedies may be sought when applicable. When these interest groups work amicably with the firm, their participation can help reduce some of the negative perceptions and confrontation that may publicly exist.

8.2   Stakeholder Analysis for QFD APPLICATION

Traditionally, the QFD team consists of members of the cross-functional units within the firm. The QFD team can be expanded to include important stakeholders. The steps to include them can be conducted as shown in Table 8-1.

Table 8-1: Stakeholder Analysis

STEP	ACTION
Step 1	Identify Stakeholders and their courses of action
Step 2	Identify the major stakeholders that can affect the competitiveness of the firm and include them in the QFD team.

Step 3	Identify stakeholders' requirements.
Step 4	Develop a list of design requirements to satisfy stakeholder requirements.
Step 5	Establish a dialog with the stakeholder teams.
Step 6	Benchmark corporate performance on the stakeholders' requirements and technical targets against those of the firm's competitors.
Step 7	Identify areas for improvement and work with stakeholders to develop a sustained plan.
Step 8	Develop a long-term association with stakeholders.
Step 9	Conduct periodic environmental scanning to determine when to add new stakeholders and when to remove inactive ones.

Steps 1: Identify the stakeholders and their courses of action

It is important to know who your stakeholders are just as it is important to know who your customers are. A comprehensive list of these stakeholders will be a beginning point as well as their courses of action. For example, how influential are these stakeholder teams? Are they likely to influence the customer perception of the product and the firm? Remember that in marketing, you do not want any negative ads. Stakeholder teams that are able to reach a wider audience and that have a track record of being on the right sides of the issue can not only influence potential customers but also legislators to enact new laws that may affect the performance of the firm. These stakeholder teams should be treated as active participants and integrated in the product planning and design stages. The list of stakeholders generated at this stage should not be static. In fact, the process of stakeholder list generation should be ongoing as new groups emerge over time and may actually have more direct impact on the firm's effectiveness.

Step 2: Identify the major stakeholders that can affect the competitiveness of the firm and include them in the QFD team.

Some of the issues in this step were discussed in step 1. However, more importantly, the firm should not be consumed with including all stakeholders in its product planning and design. In fact, this may be counter-productive and may make the firm ineffectual. It is important to analyze each stakeholder generated in step 1 and narrow the list to the significant few. There are many interest groups that are redundant and competing against each other just as in business. The focus should however, be on working with those that have the capacity to influence potential customers. The point of view or perception of influential stakeholder teams should be considered in the product planning and design stages.

Step 3: Identify stakeholders' requirements.

Once the right stakeholder teams are identified and brought into the QFD team, it is important to identify their product or service requirements. Obviously, this will focus on both the intrinsic and extrinsic values of the product or services. The requirements generated should also be evaluated to eliminate redundancies and should also be rank ordered. This will enable the firm to focus its limited resources on solving the critical requirements of the stakeholder teams. Stakeholders should also be allowed to suggest strategies to satisfy their product requirements and offer perspectives on their expectations of future outcomes.

Step 4: Develop a list of design requirements to satisfy stakeholder requirements.

The QFD team develops design requirements based on stakeholders' requirements. The design requirements should clearly outline how each of the stakeholders' requirements could be satisfied through design. Furthermore, potential tradeoffs should be identified as well as the inability to satisfy some of the stakeholders' requirements through design.

Step 5: Establish a dialog with the stakeholder teams

The QFD team should hold a dialog with stakeholder teams so both sides can understand how design requirements can be used to satisfy customer requirements. This will also help to resolve issues on tradeoffs, and infeasibility of some stakeholder requirements. In fact, this is a learning process where both sides of the aisle will understand each other's perspective better, offer different scenarios to problem solving, and develop an acceptable strategy for both parties.

***Step 6: Benchmark corporate performance on the stakeholders'
requirements and technical targets against those of the firm's
competitors.***

With a mutually acceptable design requirement to satisfy
stakeholder requirements, the process of benchmarking can begin. The
firm benchmarks itself against its major competitors. This stage is
identical to that shown in Figure 3-4.

***Step 7: Identify areas for improvement and work with stakeholders
to develop a sustained plan.***

Through benchmarking, the firm is able to position itself, assess
its strengths, weaknesses, opportunities, and threats. Furthermore, it is
able to develop capabilities where it lacks one in order to compete
effectively.

Step 8:   Develop a long-term association with stakeholders.

Long-term association with stakeholders is important. It helps the
firm obtain timely information about its environment. More
importantly, by stakeholder teams participating in making critical
product planning and design, they are more likely to accept
responsibility for the final product. This may transcend to maintaining
customer loyalty, increasing competitiveness, and assuring the
survival of the firm. It is very important that the firm seeks to work
with its active participants. These participants influence the survival of
the firm. The focus of the firm should be to design and produce the
product or service as its stakeholder groups which includes consumer
groups view as important to them and not as the designers view to be
important.

***Step 9: Conduct periodic environmental scanning to determine when
to add new stakeholders and when to remove inactive ones.***

The business environment is changing quickly. We are often
over-burdened by information overload and as more information is
made available, various people have different reactions to the
information. In return, new groups are being formed and hence, new
stakeholders emerge. Also, stakeholder groups that have achieved
their goals or are unable to follow with the dynamism of the
environment often disappear. The firm should periodically, evaluate
these stakeholder groups as to their performance in their communities.
Inactive groups should be dropped from the list and new active ones
should be added. Once the firm remains in business, it must continue
to deal with groups whose actions affect its survival.

8.3   Strategizing QFD

Our discussion on the use of stakeholders in building the QFD is strategic. We can sum this discussion up with two charts Figure 8-1 and Figure 8-2. First, we shall discuss Figure 8-1 show below.

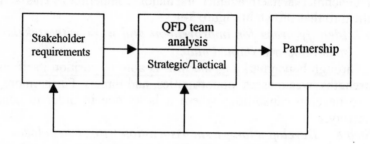

Figure 8 – 1: Stakeholder Analysis

This figure starts with information gathering. This is the process of generating information on the stakeholders, getting to know them, and integrating them in the QFD decision-making process. The stakeholders develop a list of their requirements and work with the QFD team to match design requirements against customer requirements. This takes both strategic and tactical roles. With the strategic, the firm adopts a more holistic view of its operation, links its competitiveness and survivability to the acceptance of its products or services by its stakeholders. As a result, it looks on the stakeholder to understand the key to competitiveness and survivability. The tactical phase however, deals with the actual design, planning and production. This is the responsibility of the QFD team. However, the QFD team knows that there are tradeoffs that may be involved in trying to satisfy stakeholders' requirements and also that certain requirements may not be feasible. It engages in a dialogue with the stakeholder teams on these potential tactical problems and aims to arrive at an amicable solution to this problem. Partnership is a key component of this Figure as it shows that rather than an adversarial relationship that often exists between business and interest groups, that indeed they could develop a partnership to achieve their common goals. Such partnership is good for business since it helps the two opposing views to come together, understand their different worldviews, become more pragmatic, and resolve potential conflicts productively. When these teams interact and share information, they are able to understand the different perspectives that may shape ones decision making.

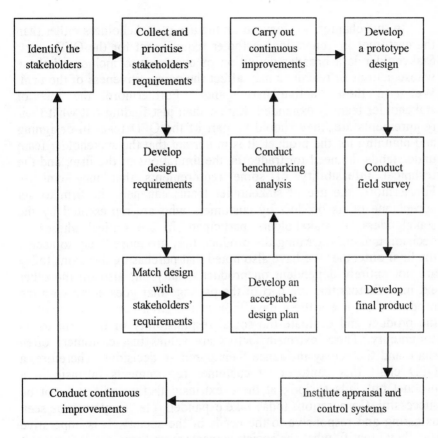

Figure 8-2: Strategic Product Planning

Figure 8-2 is an articulation of the steps outlined in Table 8-1 with the exception of the last section that starts with "Develop a prototype design." Indeed, that is the DO stage of the design process. We discussed this in chapter 6. Basically, this figure again shows that the incorporation of stakeholders in the QFD team will still make the process pragmatic but offer the added advantage that the "customer"

or "stakeholder" is directly involved in every stage of the product
design and production.

8.4   Conclusion

In this chapter, we focused on the use of stakeholders rather than
the customer in generating customer requirement for the QFD chart.
Stakeholder is a broader definition of customer to include all those
whose actions or reactions may affect the competitiveness of the firm.
We term these "active participants." Furthermore, the role of
stakeholder team is expanded. Rather than just finding out what their
requirements are, they should be part of the QFD team in designing
and planning for the product. It is important that the stakeholder team
understands the need for tradeoffs, the limitations of the firm, and the
technical infeasibility of some requirements that may emerge.
Furthermore, the use of stakeholder teams can help the firm to get
acceptance of its product by customers who are represented by the
stakeholders. If stakeholders participate in the critical phases of
decision making regarding the product, they are more likely to accept
the final outcome. We have also noted that purchasing decisions today
are not entirely dependent on product quality but also on the other
extrinsic factors that are part of the package that goes along with the
product. Customers these days look at the environmental content of
the product and evaluate the social responsibility of the firm to its
community. These extrinsic factors are values that customers often
share and these may influence their purchase decisions. Therefore, a
QFD chart that captures all customer requirements intrinsic in a
product but fails to look at these extrinsic factors will still not be
successful. Corporations today take expanded role. They must be seen
as caring and responsive to the needs of the society. It is imperative
that they identify what the society expects from them. On that note, it
is important that influential stakeholders that represent segments of
the society be part of this decision making process.

References

1. Bridis, T., "Privacy groups to boycott Intel over new chip," Associated Press, Monday, January 25, 1999.
2. Madu, C.N., and Kuei, C.H., <u>Strategic Total Quality Management</u> – *Corporate Performance and Product Quality*, Westport, CT.: Quorum Books, 1995.
3. Madu, C.N., <u>Managing Green Technologies for Global Competitiveness</u>, Westport, CT.: Quorum Books, 1996.
4. Natarajan, R. "Implementing TEQ: Steal Shamelessly from TQM," In 1993 Proceedings of Decision Sciences Institute, Vol. 3, Washington, D.C.: pp. 1870-1872.
5. Vandermerwe, S., and Oliffe, M.D., "Consumers Drive Corporations Green," Long Range Planning, 23(6): 10-16, 1990.

Chapter 9

9.0 QFD AND CONCURRENT ENGINEERING

We are witnessing the rapid proliferation of new products. Product life cycles are getting shorter. Rapid response to the market is key to competing effectively in today's market. Manufacturers are taking notice and are reacting accordingly by cutting down the time it takes to introduce new products into the market. Concurrent engineering has emerged as an approach to achieve this rapid market response. Concurrent engineering is basically, the use of a multi-disciplinary team to provide the design and development of products and processes simultaneously and rapidly. This is in response to the changing marketing environment where time management is key to improving the bottom line. Concurrent engineering takes a holistic view of the product. Rather than each department operating independently and treating their tasks in product development as independent, the different functional units within the firm work as a team and see their tasks as inter-dependent. Concurrent engineering is a business strategy where product development is done in parallel at every stage of the product development process. The focus is to make optimal use of the firm's resources. It is a shift from the traditional manufacturing processes that is vertical in nature to a horizontal process that is lateral and flat. We shall use figure 9-1 to illustrate.

9.1 Vertical vs. Horizontal Product Realization

With the vertical product realization process, the triggering point for new product development or redesigning of existing product is marketing information. The marketing department interfaces with customers or end users, obtains marketing information on customer needs and desires and relays the information to manufacturing. The need for a product is borne out of this information and the product if

83

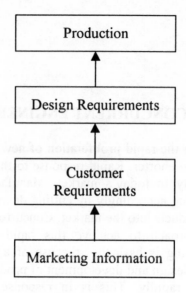

Figure 9-1: Traditional Manufacturing Process

developed must satisfy this existing need. Marketing may further organize marketing research to develop specifications for the new product, as they believe the customer may prefer. For example, what features should be in the product that will attract customer attention? Let us take for example a desktop computer. The capacity of the hard drive, the RAM, or even the inclusion of features such as IOMEGA drives or speed of the CD or even DVD may be desirable features that the customer is looking for. This is really a process of generating customer requirements as we showed in the construction of the QFD chart. Once this done, the next stage is to develop design requirements. The design requirements look at how customer requirements can be achieved through design. For example, what size of hard drive should be provided? What is the most ergonomic way to design the computer hardware? What design of keyboard will be more appropriate to satisfying customer requirement? In the QFD chart we also went through the benchmarking process. However, ones an acceptable design is developed, the next phase is production. Through the production process, a new product is developed that may satisfy the customer need. This vertical product realization process is however, very limited in some aspects. Some of the limitations are:

1. The functional departments are independent. Each department does its job and moves the next task down a sequential line. For example, the role of marketing is different from designing and designing is different from manufacturing in product conceptualization and development. Even though these departments work to achieve the overall goals of the organization, they are not unified as one body and each unit may sub-optimize and may not really understand another's perspectives and worldviews.

2. Duplication of tasks and waste are encouraged. For example, the design unit by not understanding the production system well enough may design products that may not be easily produced. Furthermore, there is backtracking of information. The product designed may not really satisfy some of the customer requirements and marketing may come back to design with a problem.

3. Quality is compromised. When there is a lack of quality in any stage of the process, the product is sent back to that phase for fixture. This creates wastes both in time of product design and production and in terms of the resources that are dedicated to the product.

4. The lead-time to introduce new product or redesigned product into the market is longer as a result of the back and forth movement between the departments, quality problems, etc. The effect of this is that with the shorter product life cycles, the firm may not be competitive in today's fast-paced marketing environment. Furthermore, production cycle time is longer as we move through this vertical chain of the product design and development.

5. Due to the long production cycle time, lower quality expected, lower efficiency of the independent departments, and slower market introduction, higher costs are incurred. Customers also expect to pay higher for the product. The firm's slow entrance into the market place implies loss of market share and lack of competitiveness.

6. Customer satisfaction is low as products may not be designed and produced right the first time around. The firm spends more time trying to rectify the problem rather than trying to continuously improve the quality of the product. Efficiency and the performance of the entire firm are affected, and manufacturing and production

costs go up. The company's market share gradually erodes as it starts to loose competitiveness.

With the problems outlined above, it is better to adopt a horizontal product realization process. This is indeed, what we achieve through concurrent engineering. Figure 9-2 is used as an illustration.

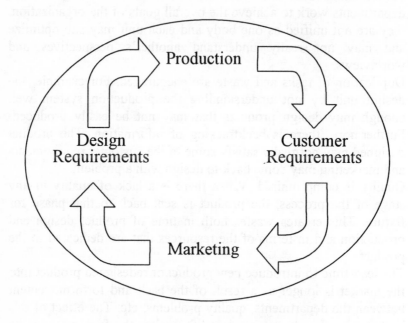

Figure 9-2: Concurrent Engineering

9.1.1   Horizontal Product Realization Process

Notice that figure 9-2 shows a flat structure for the product realization process. Each major component of product design and development as shown in Figure 9-1 is contained here. However, there is no hierarchical structure on information flow. All the functional units work in parallel; collect and analyze information the same time and make timely decisions on product design and development. The key here is that information flow is facilitated and there is ongoing interaction between members of the cross-functional units that work as a team in the product design and development. When marketing offers information on customer requirements for example, the design unit can immediately discuss the feasibility of such requirements and how they may be designed into the product. Manufacturing can evaluate the design and identify production problems or effective production strategies, finance and accounting can discuss the viability of the project and the costing. All the parties understand exactly what has to be done; where to scale down and how to improve the product design and development. More importantly, they come to understand each other and how their respective functions are inter-related and aim to achieve organizational goals. It is through such cooperation that the organization's goals and objectives are articulated. Members of the team can then work harmoniously to satisfy customer needs. The benefits of concurrent engineering are numerous. Through concurrent engineering, all the problems listed under vertical product realization process can be alleviated. In addition, the following benefits accrue:

1. Product design and development times are significantly reduced. As a result, new products can be offered to the market on a timely basis. There will be rapid response to market needs. Furthermore, existing products can be easily redesigned, upgraded, and modified in a lesser time and at lower costs to satisfy customer needs.
2. Quality is very high as products are produced right the first time. The communication and interaction between the functional units who work as concurrent engineering team members in parallel, help to ensure that problems observed at each stage of the product development can be easily resolved.
3. The key to concurrent engineering is to improve quality, reduce production cost, and reduce the delivery time of product to the market. When these goals are achieved, efficiency and performance are significantly improved. There is no backtracking as we mentioned with the vertical product realization process.
4. The firm is competitive as it responds faster to market changes. Its resources are optimized as the firm aims to satisfy its customers timely and maintain their loyalty. Thus, market shares are maintained and new markets may be gained. Customer satisfaction is high.
5. Time is effectively managed. The time to carry out tasks are cut down since redundancies and backtracking are eliminated.

9.2   QFD and Concurrent Engineering

As we have seen, concurrent engineering is actually a business strategy. It requires an overhaul of existing organizational structure to allow the functional units within the firm to operate in a team form. The concurrent engineering (CE) team or the CE team as it is often referred to as, works through the product design and development stages to ensure timely response to the dynamic market environment. The aim is to drive down costs and product development time by making optimal use of the firm's resources. Although the term concurrent engineering sounds very technical, it relies on other tools to achieve its goals. QFD is one such tool that is frequently used by CE teams. Remarkably, the goals of QFD and concurrent engineering are similar. QFD for example, uses cross-functional teams in the product development. This is also done with concurrent engineering. However, QFD as we have shown in previous chapters, can help the CE team to actually prioritize customer requirements and develop a fit between customer requirements and design requirements. Furthermore, the issue of tradeoffs and benchmarking can be better understood through the application of QFD in a concurrent engineering environment. This process however, should not be limited to the product design. In fact, concurrent engineering takes a "cradle-to-grave" approach with respect to the product. The CE team follows the product development process from the product conception to the development stage but as being done now, to the end of the product's life. It is a strategy that follows the product through its life cycle.

CE team is also not limited to the internal units within the firm. In fact, the stakeholder approach we discussed in chapter 8 is applicable here. CE team will be more effective if the team comprises of internal units as well as other stakeholders. Since the goal is to design and produce products on timely basis, it is important that stakeholders contribute to this decision-making process. As we mentioned in chapter 8, stakeholders are those who may actively influence or be influenced by the product. Therefore, the CE team should include consumer interest groups, suppliers and vendors, as well as the members of the functional units within the firm. Once the CE team is formed, QFD becomes a useful tool to help them arrive at decisions. However, it is important to understand other issues that may affect the success of concurrent engineering and the application of QFD to solve product design and development problems.

9.2.1 Successful Application of Concurrent Engineering

Concurrent engineering is a new management philosophy that interplays with a firm's business strategy. As a result, it is not easily implemented without a hitch. The success of concurrent engineering applications depends on a new attitude within the firm. It is a strategic weapon that can drive the firm to success and make it competitive but, in order to achieve all these, some hurdles must be overcome.

1. Management commitment and support – As Figure 9-2 shows concurrent engineering advocates a flat organization. This is in contrary to the hierarchical nature of both authority and information flow that exist in traditional organizations. Functional departments must be made to understand that the joint efforts of all departments are needed to make the firm more efficient and competitive. Top management developing clear missions and vision for the organization could achieve this goal. The different departments must understand their role in helping the firm achieve its goals. It should also be clear that there is no internal competition between the departments and that their activities are inter-related and synergistic. Management must support the efforts of the CE team and provide the necessary resources needed to make them effective.
2. Management involvement is required. It is not enough to support the CE team. Management should view CE team as a strategic unit and the leader of the team should be a senior executive of the firm. Yet, the CE team should be empowered to make decisions otherwise, the fast response rate expected from concurrent engineering will not be achieved.
3. CE team members should be trained appropriately on the roles of teams, problem solving and conflict resolution. Communication and sharing of information are one of the ways that conflict could be resolved. Members need to understand the different perspectives under which they operate and be open minded. Conflicts must surely arise within such a group formation. However, conflicts are not necessarily bad and can be made productive.
4. The corporate climate should be supportive of teamwork. The CE team should not be the only arm of the firm where teamwork is encouraged. In fact, the atmosphere must change to reflect a new

business strategy and a new management philosophy with the goal of transforming the organization.

5. Management practices advocated in the 1980s that contributed to the failures of Western Management styles should be examined and avoided. Deming [1] discussed these problems extensively and clearly outlined them in his 14 points. It is important that the organization takes this path if it intends to achieve success with concurrent engineering.

9.3   Conclusion

In this chapter, we discussed concurrent engineering and QFD. We noted that both aim to achieve the same goal. However, concurrent engineering is a business strategy that is based on a cross-functional team that could include stakeholders. The CE team works in parallel through product design, development, and disposition. The CE team is empowered to make timely product decisions to respond swiftly to the competitive environment. Concurrent engineering is the wave to the future in a dynamic competitive environment and operates effectively in a Total Quality Management (TQM) - based organizational culture. QFD on the other hand, is a tool that could enable the CE team to understand customer requirements, design requirements to meet customer needs into the product, and develop competitive strategies to assure successful introduction into the market. The goal here is to ensure that products of high quality are introduced timely into the market.

References

[1]   Deming, W.E., "Transformation of Western Style of Management," *Interfaces* 15(3): 6-11, 1985.
[2]   Deming, W.E., Out of the Crisis, Cambridge, Mass.: MIT Press, 1986.
[3]   Deming, W.E., The New Economics for Industry, Government, Education. Cambridge, Mass.: MIT Press, 1993.

Chapter 10

10.0   QFD, Cost Control and Productivity Improvement

Quality programs are supported only if they can help to improve the bottom-line. In all the preceding chapters, we have focused on the role of QFD in making the firm more competitive. This we stated will come about if customer satisfaction is achieved. Customers become loyal to the firm if they are satisfied. They patronize the business and spread good words about the products and services they are receiving from the firm. The business in return, will be able to increase its market share, invest in new technologies and research and development, and will be able to offer improved products and services over time. In a nutshell, the firm becomes more competitive. Yet, high quality does not necessarily mean that profits will be high. It is important to ensure that the cost of achieving high quality is kept under control. A typical example is Wallace Company, which won the coveted Malcolm Baldrige National Quality Award in 1991 but went bankrupt thereafter. Analysts have blamed the financial problems of Wallace Company on not keeping tabs on its quality costs. It is therefore imperative that any discussion about the role of quality in any business should also investigate cost control and productivity improvement issues. In this final chapter of the book, we shall tie in QFD, cost control, and productivity improvement. We shall also, borrow from the works of eminent leaders in the field of total quality management notably, Joseph M. Juran and Edward W. Deming.

10.1   Cost Control

Every successful business must have a proper control of its costs. It is generally accepted that the average cost of poor quality is in the range of 15 to 20% of total sales [1]. However, as we embark on company-wide quality management, it is difficult to keep track of the sources of these quality costs. And, if the sources of the cost of poor quality can not be isolated, it becomes difficult to control them. The lack of specificity on the sources of the cost of poor quality can distort the entire picture and lead to solving the wrong problems. Poor quality does have a significant impact on the success of the firm. It leads to increased waste of materials and resources. For example, increased number of scraps and rejects may be created, labor-hours may be used up in repeating tasks that should have been done right the first time, warranty costs and liability costs will go up, productivity will drop, and most importantly, customer dissatisfaction will be high. The effects of all these on the bottom-line are significant. For example, when customers are dissatisfied, they spread the news by word-of-mouth and raise alarm about the product or the firm. This may dissuade potential customers from purchasing the product and service. When this happens, the firm loses market share and lacks competitiveness. This impacts on the ability of the firm to continue providing products and services to its customers at a higher quality. A study by The Ernst & Young Quality Improvement Consulting Group states the following [5]:

"A potentially ... devastating consequence of the bottom line is the reaction of the customer who receives a defective or otherwise unsatisfactory product or service. A recent survey showed that, while a satisfied customer will tell a few people about his or her experience, a dissatisfied person will tell an average of 19 others."

Obviously, the word-of-mouth is a devastating tool that the customer can use to discredit a firm's product or service when he or she is dissatisfied. This study further noted that dissatisfied customers rarely complain to the provider of poor quality goods and services. Also, when they complain through the marketing or service channels, their complaints rarely get the attention they deserve. The alternative has been to switch to a competing product or service.

Many of the problems with poor quality relate to poor product or service designs and product defects. Many of these problems could have been corrected before the product gets to the customer. QFD as a tool can help ensure that product design satisfies customer requirements. As shown in chapter 9, the use of QFD and concurrent engineering can also help to eliminate defects in the product or service.

10.2   Cost of Quality (COQ)

Juran introduced the cost of quality [4]. He argues that in order to get top management to pay attention to quality, they must know the bottom-line or how poor quality affects the profit margin. Cost of quality relates to the costs to production as a result of defects or imperfection in the product. As we mentioned above, this cost could range from 15 to 20 % of the sales revenue [1]. Crosby [2] recommend that this cost should be under 2.5%. The premise behind controlling the cost of quality can be outlined as follows:
1. Prevention is cheaper than taking corrective actions. Thus, it is important to design and produce the product right the first time rather than aiming to correct defects when they do occur.
2. Performance is measurable. It is possible to measure the performance of the product or service against a metric or target specifications. The performance measures must meet or surpass the expectations of the customer.
3. Failures may result if poor quality items are designed and produced. The sources of failures can be studied, analyzed, and prevented.
There are four types of cost of quality. These are discussed below.

10.2.1 Types of cost of quality

1. Appraisal costs – this include the costs of inspection, testing, and related activities that will ensure that the final product is free of defects. Here, we see how concurrent engineering and QFD can help to eliminate appraisal costs. As noted in chapter 9, members of the CE team, work in parallel with stakeholders to ensure that the final product meets customer expectations. Defects can be eliminated through a cradle-to-grave approach of the product. For example, designers can identify design problems that could be eliminated to satisfy customer requirements. However, manufacturing may detect imperfections in the process that may contribute to defects. Material selection may also be a source of defects in the product. These sources of defects could be controlled before they occur. Inspection and testing of the product for defects could be limited if, in the design and manufacturing strategies as supported through QFD and concurrent engineering, care is taken in designing and producing the product or service.

2. Prevention costs – this cost is incurred in an attempt to prevent defects. Such costs include the cost of developing a work environment that supports the quality efforts of the organization, cost of design or redesign of the product or process, training costs, cost of the cradle-to-grave approach in manufacturing, cost of working with vendors and suppliers, cost of integrating QFD or CE teams with stakeholder teams. Prevention cost has the effect of pushing the proportion of defects down. Notice that prevention strategy involves more proactive role to control defects and manage quality. The use of QFD and CE are preventive in nature. They support the goal of producing high quality goods and services by focusing not only on design but pn all phases of production that may affect the quality of the product. For example, by working with suppliers, the manufacturer can establish a quality guideline for incoming raw materials that will be in line with the quality imperatives of the firm. When we discussed quality control in chapter 8, we noted that there are two causes of variation in a process: natural and special causes. We also noted that the operator has no control over natural causes of variation. An example of this is the selection of suppliers for raw materials. The top management makes this decision. Therefore, if the QFD team designs the right product and the suppliers send in poor quality materials to production, the firm will still not be able to satisfy customer requirements. The problem becomes systemic and only the top management can resolve it. This also highlights the importance of using concurrent engineering with QFD. It is seen here that in order to reduce the cost of poor quality, all parties that affect the product production process must participate at an early stage in developing the product. The CE team offers the opportunity of being inclusive of all significant players in the product development and production phases.

3. Internal Failure Costs – These costs deal with defects that are detected within the production system. Such include the costs of scraps, rejects and reworks before the product is shipped to the customer. These costs can be controlled if the product development stages through design and production are well guided.

4. External Failure Costs – These costs occur after the customer has received the product. This cost could be devastating to a firm. Some of the costs include warranty costs, liability costs, recall costs, loss of customer goodwill, loss of customer loyalty, complaint costs, and societal costs.

All these four types of costs can be improved on by designing quality into the product and ensuring that only products of high quality are shipped to the customer. When the customer notices defect in the product or service, it is not easily resolved by replacing the product or maintaining the warranty agreement. As we cited above, many of the complaints may not be fed back to the manufacturer but those that most matter most to the firm – customers – will come to know about the problems.

10.2.2 Views on Cost of Quality

The traditional view of cost of quality is that as prevention costs increase, the percentage defect in the product will decrease. Conversely, failure costs is directly associated with the proportion of defects. As a result, there is an optimal proportion of defects where total quality cost is minimized. This is the problem with this traditional view. It suggests that after a point, prevention is ineffective and may in fact, be costly. This may challenge the concept of continuous improvement. There are several debates about this controversial view. As expected, leading quality experts also disagree on this issue. Proponents of cost of quality are quality leaders like Juran and Crosby while Deming believed that this concept is useless.

The modern view of cost of quality is that zero defects could be achieved. This view supports a focus on prevention and argues that prevention costs are fixed while failure costs keep rising. Figures 10-1 and 10-2 show these relationships.

External and internal failure costs are estimated to account for about 60 to 90 percent of total quality costs. Traditionally, the attempt has been to increase inspection in order to reduce external failure costs. However, this could be counter-productive as it pushes up the costs of appraisal and internal failure while external failure costs may decline. It is apparent that the cost of non-conformance associated with rework, rejects, and scraps will decline as quality is continuously improved and prevention is focused on. This suggests that QFD and CE have significant role in reducing the cost of quality especially since prevention cost is a constant. By designing and producing products and services to meet customer requirements, defects can be effectively prevented if QFD and CE are concurrently used. Through CE and QFD, the number of defective items produced will be minimized thus keeping internal failure costs low; and there will be less appraisal as the products are made right the first time. Management must therefore, make the necessary commitment to support QFD and CE teams so that high quality products that meet customer requirements can be designed, developed and produced.

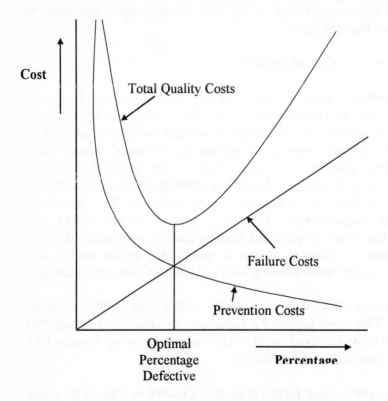

Figure 10-1: Traditional Cost of Quality

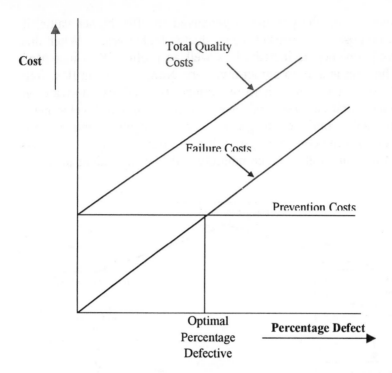

Figure 10-2. Modern Cost of Quality

10.3   Quality and Productivity Improvement

Deming [3] demonstrated a link between quality and productivity improvement. This link is often referred to as Deming's chain reaction model. We have modified the Deming chain reaction model as shown in figure 10-3. It can also be seen that we can improve the quality of the product or service through application of QFD. Quality improvement plays a significant role in the survival of a firm. For example, improvement in quality will lead to a reduction in the costs of quality we outlined above. It also, leads to higher productivity as less waste are incurred; increased customer loyalty is achieved, as customer satisfaction is higher. When the quality of the product or service is high, limited resources in terms of labor, material, and time are efficiently utilized. This will help the firm to become more competitive and gain market shares. The large market share will help the firm benefit from economies of scale and these will help to drive costs down. When the product is perceived to offer higher value, it may also be possible to market the product at higher prices. When this is achieved, revenue is increased as well as profits. With increased profits, the firm is able to attract investors. New capital can flow into the business that will help it to modernize its facilities, innovate on new products and services, and invest on research and development. The firm will continue to grow, stay in business and remain competitive. As the company grows, it also offers an important social responsibility function to its community – that of providing jobs and more jobs.

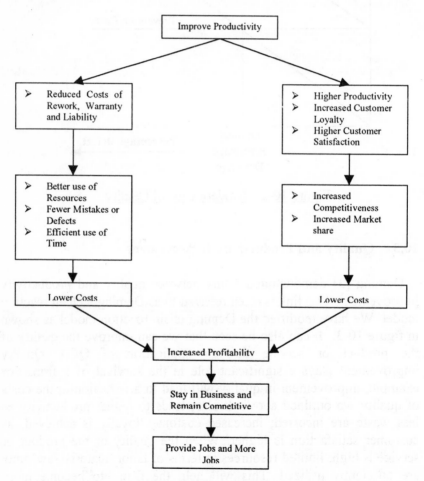

Figure 10.3: Link between Quality and Productivity

Clearly, profitability, quality and the survival of the firm go hand in hand. A firm that lacks quality products and services can not survive in today's competitive environment. Each firm must be able to define the value that its products or services offer to customers and aim to achieve quality at the highest level. QFD is emphatically, a tool that can help achieve that goal and when used concurrently with concurrent engineering, the firm is able to realize its dream of market growth.

10.4 Conclusion

In this chapter, we have discussed cost of quality and the link between quality and productivity. We have noted that offering customers products or services that satisfy their requirements may control most of the quality costs. Therefore, the QFD as a tool plays a significant role in achieving that goal. However, we have noted that concurrent engineering will be effective in conjunction with QFD since some of the problems of poor quality may not deal directly with poor designs. In fact, it is important that significant stakeholders in the CE team can help to evaluate any product design and development process and provide any necessary preventive strategies before the design and development of the product. By doing this, the cost of poor quality can be minimized. We also, contrasted the traditional and modern views of cost of quality and showed that unlike the traditional view, the prevention cost is fixed and the target is to achieve zero defects.

We ended the chapter by looking at the link between quality and productivity. We extended Deming's chain reaction model to show that in fact, improvement in quality can lead to reduction in cost of quality, higher productivity, lower costs, increased profitability, survivability and competitiveness of the firm. When the firm is competitive, it is able to expand and provide more jobs. QFD again is behind this link. It lets the manufacturer better understand its customers and to better offer products and services that will satisfy their needs. It is through QFD that quality and value can be defined into the product and services. Customer requirements can also be introduced into the product at a higher performance level but yet at lower costs if concurrent engineering team participates to develop the QFD.

References

1. Chase, R.B., and Aquilano, N.J., Production and Operations Management – Manufacturing and Services, Chicago, Ill: Irwin, 1995, 7th edition.
2. Crosby, P., Quality is Free, New York: New American Library, 1979.
3. Deming, W.E., Out of the Crisis, Cambridge, MA: MIT Center for Advanced Engineering Studies, 1986.
4. Juran, J.M., and Gryna, F.M., Juran's Quality Control Handbook, New York, NY: McGraw-Hill, 1988.
5. The Ernst & Young Quality Improvement Consulting Group, Total Quality: An Executive's Guide for the 1990s, Burr Ridge, Ill.: Irwin Professional Publishing, 1990, pp. 6-7.

Index

101

102

Index